Backyard Beekeeping Book for Beginners

A Complete Guide to Building a Thriving Beehive, Growing a Healthy Colony, and Harvesting Honey at Home

By

Elara Wrenfield

Copyright © 2025 – Elara Wrenfield
All rights reserved

No part of this publication may be reproduced, distributed, or transmitted in any form or by any means, including photocopying, recording, or other electronic or mechanical methods, without the prior written permission of the publisher, except in the case of brief quotations embodied in reviews and certain other non-commercial uses permitted by copyright law.

Disclaimer

This publication is designed to provide reliable information on the subject matter only for educational purposes, and it is not intended to provide medical advice for any medical treatment. You should always consult your doctor or physician for guidance before you stop, start, or alter any prescription medications or attempt to implement the methods discussed. This book is published independently by the author and has no affiliation with any brands or products mentioned within it. The author hereby disclaims any responsibility or liability whatsoever that is incurred from the use or application of the contents of this publication by the purchaser or reader. The purchaser or reader is hereby responsible for his or her own actions.

Table of Contents

About the Author

Elara Wrenfield is a passionate advocate for simple living, self-reliance, and reconnecting with the natural world. With a love for hands-on learning and a deep respect for the rhythms of nature, she empowers everyday people to rediscover traditional skills in a modern world — whether it's beekeeping in the backyard, growing herbs on a windowsill, or crafting a healthier, more intentional life at home.

Through her approachable and practical guides, Elara blends research-based knowledge with real-world experience, making even the most complex topics easy to understand and enjoyable to explore. Her work resonates with readers who crave clarity, connection, and confidence as they begin their journey into natural living, sustainable practices, and homegrown know-how.

When she's not writing, Elara enjoys quiet mornings with her journal, the hum of a happy garden, and finding joy in the little things — from the first sprout of the season to the clink of a home-canned jar on a pantry shelf.

Introduction

Close your eyes and picture this: a warm summer morning, the air sweet with the scent of blooming flowers, and a gentle hum rising from your backyard as honeybees dart from blossom to blossom. In the corner of your garden sits a hive—your hive—alive with purpose, productivity, and the quiet satisfaction that comes from working in harmony with nature. That, dear reader, is backyard beekeeping. And it's not just a hobby. It's a lifestyle shift, a daily dance with one of the most fascinating creatures on Earth, and yes—it's booming for a reason.

Why Beekeeping Is Buzzing Again

You might have noticed that beekeeping has gone from a fringe homesteading skill to a full-on global trend—and there's a good reason for that. Bees are essential to our food system. They pollinate over 75% of the fruits, vegetables, and nuts we eat. Without them, our plates would look alarmingly bare. But beyond their agricultural superpowers, people are rediscovering bees for something more personal: their incredible ability to connect us with nature, slow us down, and teach us patience, care, and observation.

In a world spinning ever faster—dominated by screens, stress, and supermarket shelves—beekeeping offers something radical: stillness, stewardship, and the kind of satisfaction that can't be streamed.

Whether it's the joy of harvesting your own honey, supporting pollinators, or simply falling in love with the gentle rhythm of the hive, people from all walks of life—suburban moms, urban gardeners, off-grid homesteaders, even retirees—are donning veils and lighting smokers. Beekeeping is no longer reserved for the rural or rugged. It's for anyone with a little space, a little curiosity, and a big heart for nature.

The Joy (and Responsibility) of Keeping Bees

Let's get this out of the way: beekeeping is magical… but it's also a commitment. These aren't houseplants you can ignore for a week. A hive is a living, breathing super-organism made up of tens of thousands of individual bees working in perfect coordination. They're not pets—but they're not wild animals either. They are partners in the truest sense. You'll be learning their needs, anticipating their behaviors, and yes, sometimes making mistakes along the way.

You'll witness tiny eggs become workers, see nectar transformed into golden honey, and maybe even catch your bees preparing to swarm—a heart-racing spectacle no beekeeper forgets. But with this joy comes responsibility: to care for your bees through every season, to protect them from pests and diseases, and to do your part in keeping their species—and our food systems—thriving.

Don't worry—we're going to walk through all of it together. No jargon. No intimidation. Just clear, practical, down-to-earth beekeeping you can actually do.

How This Book Will Guide You from Start to Success

This isn't just a manual—it's your beekeeping blueprint. Whether you've got a city rooftop, a backyard garden, or a country acre, this book is designed to meet you right where you are and walk you step-by-step from beginner to confident beekeeper.

We'll start with the bee basics: how hives work, the types of bees, and what makes them so essential to our ecosystem. Then we'll dive into choosing your hive, gathering your gear, and sourcing your first colony. You'll learn how to care for your bees throughout the year, how to recognize signs of trouble (and what to do about them), and eventually, how to harvest your own honey—ethically and joyfully.

Along the way, you'll also discover how to make your garden more pollinator-friendly, how to avoid common rookie mistakes, and how to grow your passion into something truly rewarding.

And don't worry—every chapter is packed with tips, and real talk about what to expect. No fluff, no filler, and definitely no sugarcoating.

What You'll Need—And What You Don't—To Begin

Here's the good news: you don't need a farm, a fortune, or a Ph.D. in entomology to start keeping bees. You don't even need a huge backyard. What you *do* need is a little space (a sunny, wind-protected spot works great), a willingness to learn, and a sense of respect for these tiny powerhouses.

Yes, you'll need some basic equipment—like a hive, a bee suit, and a smoker—but we'll walk through exactly what to get in the coming chapters. You won't be pressured into overbuying or overwhelmed with technicalities. This book was written to simplify, not complicate.

By the time you finish reading, you'll know what kind of bees to start with, how to set up a healthy hive, and how to support your colony through the seasons. You'll feel confident, informed, and ready to begin—not someday, but *this season*.

So if you've ever dreamed of bottling your own honey, watching bees work in your backyard, or simply doing something deeply meaningful and earth-friendly—this is your moment.

Get your gloves ready. Strike your smoker. The hive is waiting.

Let's go meet your bees.

Chapter 1

Understanding Bees & Their Behavior

Meet the hive mind in action

Now that you're officially stepping into the world of beekeeping, it's time to meet the stars of the show: **the bees themselves**. Beekeeping isn't just about honey—it's about understanding a living, buzzing super-organism. A beehive isn't just a box full of insects. It's a carefully choreographed, complex society where every single bee has a job, a purpose, and a mission. This chapter is your all-access pass to how a colony works, thrives—and sometimes, fails.

The Hive Cast: Queen, Workers & Drones

If a beehive were a kingdom, you'd naturally assume the queen rules over it all. But here's the twist: although she wears the crown, she doesn't issue orders. She doesn't command her workers or assign jobs. Instead, she plays a more subtle yet absolutely vital role—like the beating heart of the colony—while the real day-to-day work is carried out by tens of thousands of her daughters: the **worker bees**.

A honeybee colony is a **super-organism**—meaning all its members function like parts of one single body. The queen, workers, and drones each have very specific roles that keep the hive alive and thriving. And understanding what each of them does is the foundation of becoming a skilled and responsible beekeeper.

The Queen Bee: Mother of the Colony

There is **only one queen bee** in a healthy hive, and her entire life revolves around reproduction. She is noticeably **larger and longer** than the other bees, with a smooth, elongated abdomen that extends well past her wings.

The queen is born from the same type of egg as any other female bee, but she's fed **royal jelly**—a nutrient-rich secretion—from the moment her egg hatches. This special diet alters her development, triggering hormones that turn her into a fully fertile queen instead of a sterile worker.

Her primary job? **Lay eggs.** And lots of them—up to **1,500 to 2,000 eggs per day** during the peak season. That's more than her body weight in eggs daily! She lays each egg into an individual hexagonal cell in the comb, and depending on what the colony needs, she'll lay **fertilized eggs** (which become female workers or potential queens) or **unfertilized eggs** (which develop into male drones).

8

But egg-laying isn't all she does.

The queen also produces a unique **pheromone**—a chemical scent called the **Queen Mandibular Pheromone (QMP)**—that spreads through the hive via contact with worker bees. This "queen scent" tells the colony she is healthy, active, and present. It keeps the workers from rearing a new queen and helps regulate overall colony behavior and harmony.

If the queen becomes weak, injured, or dies, the hive will begin **emergency queen rearing**—turning a freshly laid egg into a replacement queen. It's one of the most fascinating survival mechanisms in nature.

The Worker Bees: The Unsung Heroines

Worker bees are **sterile females**, and they make up **about 99%** of the hive's population. A single hive can house between **20,000 to 60,000** workers at peak season. Despite being smaller than the queen, their importance can't be overstated—**they literally do everything.**

What's even more amazing is that a worker bee's role **changes with age** in a well-defined sequence known as **age polyethism**. Here's a rough breakdown of her job progression over her short, 6-week lifespan (in warm seasons):

Days 1–3: Cell Cleaner

She cleans the wax cells, preparing them to receive new eggs or food.

Days 4–11: Nurse Bee

She feeds and tends to larvae and the queen, producing royal jelly from special glands.

Days 12–17: Builder, Wax Maker, and Comb Maintainer

She secretes wax from glands and helps build the honeycomb. She also regulates hive temperature by fanning her wings.

Days 18–21: Guard Bee

She guards the hive entrance, identifying intruders and defending the colony from threats.

Day 22 onward: Forager

She ventures outside to collect nectar, pollen, propolis, and water—bringing resources back to the hive.

During this final stage, a worker bee faces the most danger. From predators to weather, every trip outside shortens her already brief life.

Worker bees also:

- **Dehydrate nectar into honey** by fanning it with their wings
- **Cap honey and brood cells** with wax
- **Regulate hive temperature** year-round
- **Remove dead bees and waste** from the hive (yes, they have undertakers!)

In short, the hive wouldn't last a single day without its relentless, selfless workforce of worker bees.

The Drones: The Romantic, Short-Lived Males

Drones are the **male bees** of the colony, and they have a single, dramatic purpose: to **mate with a virgin queen** during her nuptial flight.

They are larger than worker bees, with **thicker bodies, bigger eyes**, and **no stinger**. Unlike workers, drones:

- Do **not** collect nectar or pollen
- Do **not** make wax or clean cells
- Do **not** guard the hive
- Do **not** contribute to daily labor

They essentially lounge around the hive, consuming resources, until mating season comes.

During this period, drones fly out to **drone congregation areas**, where they wait in swarms for virgin queens to pass through. If they manage to mate with a queen mid-air, the act is **fatal**—their endophallus is torn from their bodies, and they die immediately after.

Those who don't mate? They're often **kicked out of the hive** in autumn, just before winter, when resources become scarce. The hive simply can't afford to feed non-working members during the cold months.

Though their role seems limited, drones are **genetically important**. Since they're born from unfertilized eggs, they carry only the queen's genetics, but their role in queen fertilization ensures genetic diversity across colonies.

Queen	Worker	Drone
Egg Laying	Food & Hive Care	Mating

Hive Caste Comparison

The Honeybee Life Cycle

Every honeybee in the hive—whether she becomes a worker, a drone, or a queen—starts the same way: as a tiny egg laid by the queen. But what happens after that is a **beautifully orchestrated transformation**, unfolding in **four key stages: egg, larva, pupa, and adult**.

What's truly fascinating is that a bee's *role* in the hive isn't determined by its genes, but by what it's **fed** in its earliest days. All bees start the same—but queens are made, not born.

Let's walk through each stage day by day:

Days 1–3: The Egg Stage

The queen moves from cell to cell inside the hive, laying one egg into each hexagonal wax cell. These eggs are about the size of a grain of rice and stand upright. They're nearly invisible to the untrained eye!

Depending on the queen's needs and the condition of the colony, she may lay:

- **Fertilized eggs** – which become **female bees** (workers or queens)
- **Unfertilized eggs** – which become **male bees** (drones)

Days 4–6: The Larva Stage

After three days, the egg hatches into a tiny, white **larva**. It looks like a curled-up grub lying at the bottom of the cell. At this point, the real work begins—**nurse bees** immediately start feeding the larva.

11

- For the first few days, all larvae are fed **royal jelly**, a protein-rich secretion made by worker bees.
- Around Day 4 or 5, if the larva is destined to become a **worker or drone**, its diet shifts to **bee bread** (a mix of pollen and nectar).
- If it's chosen to become a **queen**, it continues receiving royal jelly exclusively for the entire larval phase. This special diet triggers the full development of her ovaries and changes her body structure entirely.

During this stage, the larva **grows rapidly**, shedding its skin several times.

Days 7–14: The Pupa Stage

Once the larva is fully grown, worker bees **cap the cell with wax**. Inside, the larva spins a delicate cocoon around itself and enters the **pupal** stage.

This is when the real transformation begins—just like a caterpillar becoming a butterfly.

- Legs, wings, eyes, and fuzzy hairs start to develop.
- Its soft body darkens and hardens.
- By the end of this stage, the once-grub-like larva has transformed into a fully formed bee.

Days 15–21: The Adult Bee Emerges

Around **day 21**, the new adult bee **chews her way out** of the wax cap and emerges from the cell—fully formed and ready to work.

- **Worker bees** take about 21 days to develop.
- **Drones** (males) usually take **24 days**.
- **Queens**, fueled by royal jelly, develop fastest—emerging in just **16 days**.

Once emerged:

- Worker bees begin their life inside the hive doing nurse duties, eventually graduating to foraging outside.
- Drones begin preparing for mating flights.
- A new queen will fight rival queens to the death before taking her place on the throne.

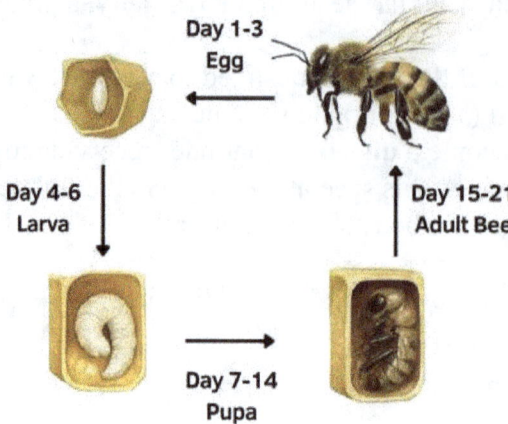

Day 1-3
Egg

Day 4-6
Larva

Day 15-21
Adult Bee

Day 7-14
Pupa

How Bees Talk: Dance, Scent & Vibes

Bees don't talk—but they sure know how to communicate.

Honeybees live in complete darkness inside the hive. Yet, they work together like a well-tuned orchestra, raising young, making wax, storing food, and responding to danger without a single spoken word. Their secret? A complex and fascinating system of **movement, scent, and vibrations**.

Let's break it down:

The Waggle Dance

If there's a honeybee version of Google Maps, this is it.

When a **forager bee** finds a good source of nectar or pollen, she doesn't just return to the hive and hope the others figure it out. She **performs a dance**—literally. This behavior, called the **waggle dance**, was first discovered by Austrian scientist **Karl von Frisch** and is still one of the most remarkable communication systems in the animal kingdom.

Here's how it works:

- The bee runs in a figure-eight pattern on the comb.
- In the middle, she **waggles her body** while moving in a straight line.
- The **angle** of the waggle line shows the direction of the food source in relation to the **sun**.
- The **duration and intensity** of the waggle tells how far away it is.

So if she wiggles in a line pointing 30° to the right of vertical, she's saying, "Fly 30° to the right of the sun!" If she waggles vigorously, the food source is rich. Less enthusiasm? It's still worth checking, but maybe not urgent.

13

Yes—**bees do trigonometry.** Naturally. No math class needed.

Pheromones

Bees also communicate through **pheromones**, which are chemical signals they release to influence the behavior of other bees.

Think of pheromones like invisible texts sent through smell.

Some common types:

- **Alarm pheromones**: Released when a bee stings or feels threatened. It smells a bit like bananas! Other bees pick it up and rush to defend the hive.
- **Nasonov pheromone**: Used to mark home. For example, when a swarm is relocating, some bees raise their abdomens and **fan their wings**, releasing this pheromone to help others find the new hive location.
- **Queen pheromone**: Produced by the queen to let everyone know she's alive and healthy. It keeps the workers from raising a new queen and helps organize hive behavior.

Without pheromones, the hive would fall into chaos. They're essential to hive coordination and social structure.

Vibrations

Honeybees also use **vibrations** to send signals through the hive's comb. Inside the dark, crowded hive, this is one of the most effective ways to get a message across.

Bees vibrate their bodies or **beat their wings** rapidly for different reasons:

- **Fanning**: To cool the hive or evaporate water from nectar while making honey.
- **Shaking or buzzing**: A form of "wake-up call" from one bee to another, often used to stimulate foraging or work.
- **Piping**: A rare sound made by queens during swarming or emergence. It's like a call of challenge or readiness.

In essence, bees use vibrations like **invisible phone calls**, felt rather than heard.

What Makes a Colony Thrive or Collapse

A healthy hive is a **delicate, living system**. Everything must be in balance: enough bees, a productive queen, stable temperature, available forage, and protection from disease and pests. When even one piece goes missing or gets disrupted, things can go wrong—fast.

Here's what makes a **colony thrive**:

- A healthy, egg-laying **queen bee**
- Abundant **worker bees** to forage, build, and care for young
- Clean, **well-ventilated combs**
- Easy access to **nectar and pollen**
- Protection from predators, pests, and weather

And here's what causes **collapse**:

- **Queen failure** – If the queen dies, stops laying, or goes missing and isn't replaced, the colony can't survive. No queen = no future bees.
- **Pests and parasites** – Especially **varroa mites**, which latch onto bees and transmit deadly viruses.
- **Starvation** – If flowers are scarce or nectar flow dries up, the hive can run out of food.
- **Overcrowding or poor management** – Bees need space and cleanliness. An overcrowded or neglected hive can trigger swarming, disease, or fighting.
- **Pesticide exposure** – Some pesticides can kill bees instantly or disrupt their navigation and memory, leading to **colony collapse disorder (CCD)**.

You'll learn later in the book how to prevent all these issues—but remember: **a proactive, observant beekeeper is the colony's best chance at survival**.

Wild Bees vs. Managed Honeybees

Before you assume all bees live in wooden boxes and make honey, let's zoom out.

There are over **20,000 known species** of bees on Earth. Most of them are **wild** and live without human interference. Honeybees (Apis mellifera) are just one species—and a managed one at that.

Wild Bees

- Usually **solitary**, meaning they don't live in colonies
- Nest in the **ground**, hollow stems, trees, or abandoned burrows
- Often **specialize** in pollinating specific native plants
- Don't make harvestable honey—but are **essential pollinators**
- Examples: **Bumblebees, Mason Bees, Leafcutter Bees**

They don't produce honey for us, but without them, many native plants would struggle to survive.

Managed Honeybees

- Live in **large colonies** of 20,000–60,000 bees
- Are **domesticated** and maintained by beekeepers
- Make large amounts of honey and **wax**

- Are widely used in **agriculture** for crop pollination
- Can be transported in hives to **support farms and orchards**

Both wild and managed bees play a role in keeping our planet green and fed.

Wild Bees   **Managed Honeybees**

Fun facts…

- A single bee produces only about **1/12 teaspoon** of honey in her lifetime. That makes every drop a marvel.
- Bees can recognize **human faces**. They process visual info similarly to us.
- The hive is kept at a precise **93°F (34°C)** year-round, even in winter!
- Bees beat their wings **200 times per second**—that's where the hum comes from.
- Honey never spoils. Archaeologists have found pots of it in Egyptian tombs that were still edible!

Wrapping up…

Before you put on your veil and light your smoker, take a moment to appreciate the brilliance of the bees. What you're stepping into isn't just a hobby—it's a relationship with one of the most fascinating social creatures on the planet.

Now that you know how the hive works, it's time to prepare your space, your gear, and your mindset for the journey ahead.

Chapter 2

Planning Your Backyard Apiary

Finding the perfect home for your bees

You've met the bees, marveled at their tiny genius, and now you're officially itching to get started. But before you rush off to buy your first hive, take a deep breath. First things first: where exactly are your bees going to live?

Choosing the right location for your hive is one of the most important decisions you'll make as a beekeeper. Think of it like house-hunting—except for 50,000 roommates. A good spot will make life easier for you and healthier for your bees. A bad one? Well, let's not go there.

This chapter helps you plan the perfect setup, whether you're working with a backyard, rooftop, balcony, or even a small rural plot.

Choosing the Best Spot for Your Hive

Think of this like real estate for bees: **location is everything**.

Where you place your hive directly affects bee health, productivity, and your own success as a beekeeper. A well-placed hive will:

- Stay drier and warmer
- Be easier to manage
- Produce more honey
- Keep your bees less defensive

Let's break it down.

Morning Sunlight is a Must

Bees wake up with the sun. Hives facing the morning sun (ideally **southeast**) warm up faster, encouraging earlier foraging and better productivity throughout the day. The warmth also helps prevent moisture buildup and disease in cooler months.

Avoid Deep Shade

A little afternoon shade is okay, especially in hot climates. But **too much shade** can result in:

- Dampness inside the hive
- Mold or mildew
- Lethargic bees
- Lower honey yield

Keep the Hive Off the Ground

Elevate your hive on cinder blocks, a wooden stand, or a purpose-built hive base. Benefits:

- Prevents ground moisture from seeping in
- Discourages pests like ants or small mammals
- Makes inspections easier on your back

Sunlight, Wind & Natural Barriers

Sunlight: Full vs. Partial Exposure

In cooler climates, aim for **full sun exposure** to keep your bees active and reduce internal hive moisture. In hotter regions, **afternoon shade** from trees or structures can prevent overheating.

Wind Protection: Natural Shields

Bees prefer calm, stable environments. **Strong winds** stress the colony and interfere with their flight paths. Position your hive near:

- A hedge
- A row of shrubs
- A privacy fence
- A garden shed

But be careful—don't **trap** your bees. Good **airflow** is just as essential. Think of it like this: protect from wind, not from air.

How Much Space Do You Really Need?

One of the biggest myths in beekeeping is that you need lots of land. In reality, you need just enough room to:

- Walk behind and beside your hive (you'll always open it from the back)
- Safely remove hive parts (like supers or frames)
- Stand clear of the bees' **flight path** (they exit straight out the front)

Absolute Minimum:

- **3 feet x 3 feet** of clear space around the hive
- **3 feet** of clearance in front of the entrance

Ideal for Comfort:

- **6 feet x 6 feet** with a clear view of the hive
- Room for a second hive if you expand (and you probably will!)

Also important:

- Avoid placing hives near **high traffic zones** (doors, patios, playgrounds)
- Make sure your bees' flight path doesn't head directly into neighbors' yards

Backyard, Rooftop, or Balcony

No backyard? No problem. Bees are adaptable—as long as **you** meet their needs.

Backyard

Ideal for beginners. Offers easy access, natural forage, and often fewer logistical challenges. Great for families and hobbyists.

Rooftop

- Surprisingly effective in urban settings!
- Bees forage up to 3 miles, so they'll find flowers.
- You'll need:
    - **Sturdy access** (no narrow fire escapes!)
    - **Wind barriers**
    - **Water source nearby**

Also check for:

- Building codes
- Structural limits (a full hive can weigh over 100 lbs with honey)
- Permission if you rent

Balcony

Possible, but challenging. You must:

- Secure the hive so it doesn't tip
- Ensure bees' flight path doesn't cross neighbors or windows
- Provide **a clean, nearby water source**

- Shield from wind and excessive sun

For very tight spaces, consider **mini hives** like Top-Bar or Warre formats.

Local Rules & Regulations

Just because you *can* keep bees doesn't mean you can do so *anywhere, anyhow*. Many areas have regulations that protect both bees and neighbors.

Before placing your hive, check with:

- Your **city or county zoning office**
- Your **state Department of Agriculture**
- Your **Homeowner's Association (HOA)**

Typical rules might include:

- Minimum distance from property lines or buildings
- Maximum number of hives allowed
- Fencing requirements (especially if the hive is near a sidewalk)
- Providing a constant **water source**

Pro Tip:

Keep a printout of your local regulations in your bee journal or binder—you'll want it handy in case someone questions your setup.

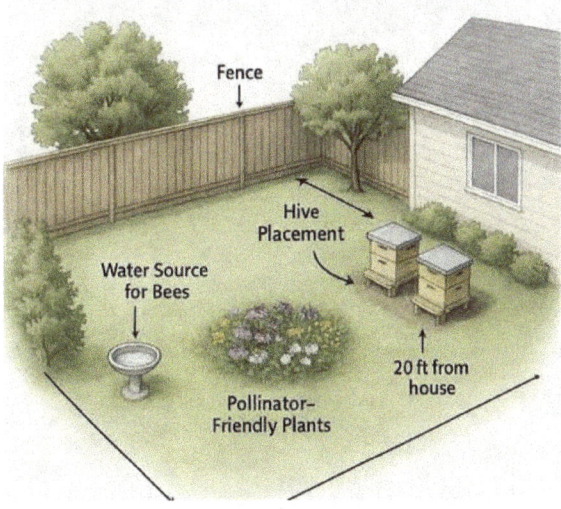

Bee Friendly Zoning

Talking to Neighbors

Bees tend to mind their own business—but your neighbors might not.

Approaching your neighbors with transparency and kindness is a smart move, especially if:

- They have young children
- Someone is allergic
- You share a property line

How to Start the Conversation:

- Emphasize how **non-aggressive** honeybees are
- Explain you're a **registered, responsible** beekeeper
- Reassure them about **safety practices** (fencing, water, hive placement)
- Offer a future **jar of honey**—it's a sweet way to earn goodwill

If someone is concerned, listen carefully. Ask questions. Most fear comes from **wasps or hornets**, not honeybees. Once they understand, they're often relieved—and sometimes fascinated.

Wrapping up…

You've now got the tools to choose the perfect hive location, avoid legal headaches, and keep the peace with your neighbors.

You've also learned that **beekeeping doesn't require a farm—just a thoughtful setup** and a commitment to doing things right.

Chapter 3

Hive Types, Equipment & Tools

Now that you've picked the perfect spot for your backyard apiary, it's time to build—or buy—your bees a place to live. In this chapter, you'll discover everything you need to know about **hives, tools, protective gear**, and even how to set up on a budget.

You don't need a fancy workshop or expensive gear to get started. But you do need to understand the essentials. Think of this as your **beekeeping toolbox starter guide**—packed with the what, why, and how much.

Choosing the Right Hive

Your bees need a place to call home—and you need a setup that fits your space, goals, and comfort level.

All beehives serve the same core function: to **protect your colony, house the queen and brood**, and give bees a secure space to **store nectar and turn it into honey**.

But how that home is designed can make a big difference in how *you* manage your bees—and how they behave.

As a beginner, you'll want to choose a hive that matches your:

- Physical strength and comfort
- Space available
- Interest in honey harvesting
- Desired level of hands-on involvement

Let's explore the **three most common hive types** used by backyard beekeepers. Each has its own design, benefits, and trade-offs.

Langstroth Hive – *The Most Popular Choice*

The **Langstroth hive** is the most widely used design among hobbyists and commercial beekeepers alike. If you've ever seen photos or videos of stacked white boxes with bees flying in and out—this is it.

How it works:

Langstroth hives are built from a series of **stacked rectangular boxes**, each containing **removable wooden frames**. Bees build their comb within these frames. The bottom boxes are where the queen lays eggs (the **brood chamber**), while the upper boxes are used for **honey storage** (called **supers**).

Pros:

- Standard design: **easier to find supplies and replacement parts**
- Built for honey: maximizes **honey production and extraction**
- Modular: you can **add or remove boxes** as your hive grows
- Designed for inspections: easy to monitor colony health

Cons:

- **Heavy lifting** involved—boxes full of honey can weigh 40–60 lbs
- Less natural for the bees (more human-centered design)
- Requires more frequent inspections and maintenance

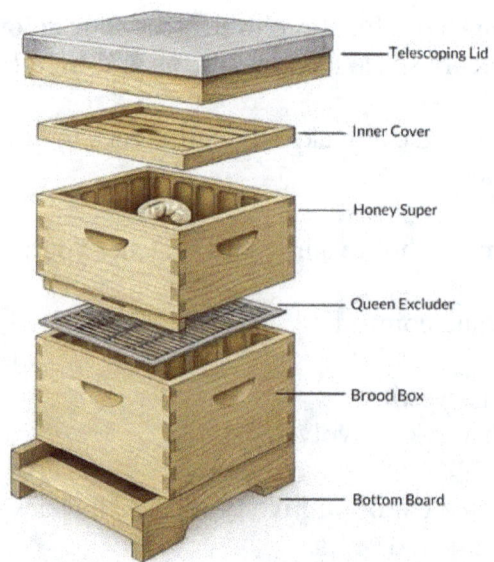

Telescoping Lid

Inner Cover

Honey Super

Queen Excluder

Brood Box

Bottom Board

Langstroth Hive

Top-Bar Hive – *Horizontal, Natural, and Simple*

The **Top-Bar hive** looks very different from the Langstroth. Instead of stacked boxes, it's a long, horizontal box (similar to a trough or open barrel) with simple wooden **bars laid across the top**. Bees hang their comb **freely from each bar**, without frames or foundation.

This hive is especially popular among **natural beekeepers**, educators, and people who want a low-lifting alternative.

How it works:
Bees draw natural comb from each top bar. You inspect the colony by lifting one bar at a time, which can be gentler on the bees. The hive doesn't require heavy lifting since there are **no stacked boxes**.

Pros:

- No lifting of stacked boxes = **easy on the back**
- Encourages **natural bee behavior** and comb building
- Ideal for **observation**, education, and gentle interaction
- Lower cost to build (great for DIY beekeepers)

Cons:

- Harder to **extract large quantities of honey**
- No standard sizing = **limited availability** of commercial parts
- Not ideal if you're aiming to grow beyond 1–2 hives

Top-Bar Hive

Warre Hive – *Vertical, Minimalist, and Bee-Centered*

Pronounced "wah-RAY," the **Warre hive** is inspired by the way bees naturally nest in **hollow trees**. It's vertical like the Langstroth but **simpler and more hands-off**. Instead of adding boxes to the top, you **add new boxes to the bottom**—mimicking how bees expand downward in the wild.

How it works:
Each box has **top bars** (like the top-bar hive), and the bees build comb naturally down from them. Beekeepers avoid disturbing the colony by doing fewer inspections and only harvesting honey from the top boxes.

Pros:

- **Low-maintenance** and less intrusive
- Keeps bees calm by **minimizing human interference**
- Mimics **natural hive behavior**
- Excellent for those focused on bee health over honey quantity

Cons:

- **Less honey** is harvested
- Not ideal for regular inspections
- Harder to find parts and equipment compared to Langstroth
- Requires **lifting the entire hive** to add a new box underneath

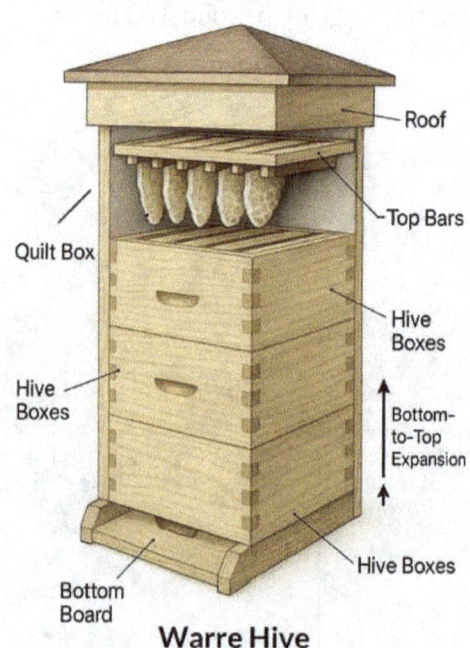

Warre Hive

Which Hive Is Right for You?

Hive Type	Best For	Avoid If You Want...
Langstroth	Maximum honey, standard setup	A lightweight or minimalist option

| Top-Bar | Natural feel, gentle inspection, DIY vibe | High honey yield or expansion |
| Warre | Hands-off approach, naturalistic beekeeping | Frequent management or inspections |

Pro Tip for Beginners

If you're unsure, **start with a single Langstroth hive**. It's widely supported, easy to learn with, and gives you the flexibility to grow or pivot later. Once you're more experienced, you can experiment with other styles based on your goals and philosophy.

Hive Components: What's What?

No matter what hive style you eventually choose—Langstroth, Top-Bar, or Warre—the basic idea is the same: **create a safe, organized environment where bees can raise their young and store food.** While the shape and layout may vary slightly, most hive systems have similar essential components.

Here's a breakdown of the **key parts** of a standard Langstroth hive—the most common and beginner-friendly hive type.

Core Components of a Hive (from bottom to top)

1. Bottom Board

This is the **foundation of the hive**, quite literally. It's the flat base everything else rests on. It also serves as the **main entrance and exit** for your bees.

- Comes in solid or screened versions (screened helps with ventilation and pest control).
- Elevates the hive off the ground, protecting it from dampness and pests.

2. Entrance Reducer

This is a **removable wooden or plastic strip** that fits in the hive entrance. It adjusts the size of the opening to suit the season or colony strength.

- Keeps robbing bees, wasps, and mice out.
- Reduces airflow in winter to help maintain warmth.

3. Brood Box (or Deep Super)

This is where the **magic happens**. The queen lays her eggs here, and young bees are raised in the comb cells. It's also where worker bees store pollen and some honey for feeding the brood.

- Usually the lowest box in the hive stack.
- Contains **frames** (typically 8–10) for comb building.

4. Frames

These are the **removable wooden rectangles** inside each box where bees build their comb.

- Bees use wax to create hexagonal cells on the frames.
- Some frames come with wax foundation to guide the bees.
- Frames in the brood box will contain eggs, larvae, pollen, and some honey.

Pro Tip: Learning how to pull and inspect frames is a key beekeeping skill you'll master early on.

5. Honey Supers

These are **shallower boxes** stacked above the brood box. Bees use them strictly for **storing surplus honey**—the kind you'll eventually harvest!

- Each super also contains 8–10 frames.
- You can add multiple supers as your colony grows and nectar flows.

Fun fact: One full honey super can weigh **30–40 lbs** when filled with capped honey!

6. Inner Cover

This sits directly under the outer lid. It helps with **temperature control, moisture regulation**, and provides a **top entrance** if needed.

- Some designs have a central hole for extra ventilation or feeding.

7. Outer Cover (Telescoping Lid)

This is the **weatherproof "roof"** of the hive. It protects everything below it from **rain, wind, sun, and snow.**

- Most outer covers are made of wood with a metal top for durability.
- Designed to extend beyond the sides of the hive to channel water away.

Essential Beekeeping Tools

What you really need—and why

When you're first starting out, it's easy to feel like you need every shiny tool in the catalog. The good news? You really don't. Beekeeping doesn't require a workshop full of gadgets. In fact, you can get started with just a few well-chosen essentials that will keep **you safe**, **your bees calm**, and **your hive accessible**.

Here's a breakdown of the core tools every beginner beekeeper should have—and what they're actually used for.

Hive Tool

Your #1 must-have item.

This small, flat metal bar is the backbone of your toolkit. Bees seal their hive boxes and frames with **propolis**—a sticky, resin-like glue made from tree sap. It makes the hive secure, but also difficult to open. The hive tool helps you:

- Pry apart boxes and lids
- Loosen and lift sticky frames
- Scrape off excess wax or propolis buildup
- Gently lift or nudge comb without damage

Think of it as the beekeeper's version of a crowbar, scraper, and lever—all in one. **Never open a hive without it.**

Smoker

For calming your bees—without harm.

A smoker is a canister-like device that lets you puff cool smoke into the hive entrance and between frames. But don't worry—it's not to scare or hurt your bees. Here's what it actually does:

- Masks **alarm pheromones**, which bees release when they sense a threat
- Distracts bees by triggering their instinct to gorge on honey (in case of fire)
- Keeps the colony calm while you inspect or harvest

Use natural materials like pine needles, wood pellets, or cardboard for clean, cool smoke. Avoid using any synthetic materials or treated wood—these can be toxic to bees.

Bee Brush

Gentle and useful for clearing bees safely.

Sometimes you'll need to gently move bees off of frames, tools, or surfaces. A bee brush is designed just for that—its soft, flexible bristles allow you to:

- Move bees without harming their delicate bodies
- Avoid swatting or blowing, which stresses the colony
- Clear bees off of frames before inspecting, replacing, or harvesting

It's especially handy during honey harvest or when transferring frames between boxes.

Pro tip: Use with care—over-brushing can irritate bees. A few light strokes usually do the trick.

Frame Grip *(Optional, but helpful)*

Like a pair of bee-safe tongs.

If you have trouble gripping frames—especially when they're stuck down with wax or heavy with honey—a frame grip is a lifesaver. It lets you:

- Lift frames straight up without tilting
- Reduce disturbance to nearby bees
- Avoid accidentally dropping a frame (which can cause chaos)

It's not essential, but beginners often find it useful while getting the hang of things.

When you're first starting out in beekeeping, one of the biggest concerns you'll probably have is the same thing that crosses everyone's mind: **"What if I get stung?"**

Let's be clear—**honeybees are not naturally aggressive**. They're peaceful, focused workers who only sting when they feel their colony is under threat. But here's the thing: when you're opening up their hive, removing frames, and making changes in their world, it's easy for a few bees to feel alarmed. And a startled beginner—especially after a first sting—can panic, flinch, or drop equipment, which only agitates the bees further.

That's why **wearing the right protective gear is one of the smartest things you can do in your early days as a beekeeper**. It gives you the confidence to move slowly and calmly, which helps you stay safe—and helps your bees stay chill, too.

Protective Gear

Here's a breakdown of what you'll need—and why each piece matters.

Bee Suit or Beekeeping Jacket

- A **full-body suit** covers you from head to ankle and includes a **built-in veil** to protect your face and neck.

- Usually made from thick cotton or synthetic material, it's designed to prevent stingers from reaching your skin.
- If a full suit feels too much, a **beekeeping jacket** with a veil is a lighter alternative that still covers your upper body and head—where most stings happen.

Beginner Tip: If you're nervous or working a new hive, choose the full suit. The peace of mind is worth it.

Veil (Your #1 Must-Have!)

- Bees are most likely to sting around the **face and neck**, which are also the most sensitive and dangerous places to get stung.
- A veil is your **non-negotiable** protection. Whether it's part of your suit or separate, always wear it during inspections.
- It allows full visibility while creating a physical barrier between you and any curious or defensive bees.

Gloves

- Protect your **hands and wrists**, which are the most used and most exposed parts during hive inspections.
- **Leather gloves** offer strong protection, though they can be bulky.
- **Fabric gloves** (with rubber coating) provide more dexterity and still guard against stings.
- Some experienced beekeepers go bare-handed for better control—but that's *much* later in your journey.

Beginner tip: Stick with gloves for now. Better grip and less anxiety = a better experience for you and your bees.

Boots or High Socks

- Bees are surprisingly sneaky—and curious.
- Without proper coverage, they might crawl **up your pant legs** (ask any seasoned beekeeper how *that* feels).
- **Boots** that go above the ankle are ideal.
- If you're wearing sneakers or loose pants, tuck them into **thick socks** or wrap them with rubber bands to seal the openings.

Pro tip:

As you get more comfortable around your bees, you might find you don't need the full setup every time. Some long-time beekeepers work with **just a veil and gloves**—or even bare-faced (not recommended for beginners!). But in your **first year**, it's wise to **suit up completely** for every hive check. The extra protection keeps you focused and confident, which your bees will appreciate.

Veil

Gloves——

——Bee Suit

Boots——

Budgeting for Your First Season

Start smart—spend wisely

Let's talk money. One of the first questions new beekeepers ask is, *"How much is this going to cost me?"* And the honest answer is: **less than you think—if you plan wisely.**

Beekeeping can be as affordable or as expensive as you make it. Sure, there are upfront costs, but once you've got your essentials in place, ongoing expenses are relatively low. And remember: unlike most hobbies, this one can literally pay you back—in honey!

Below is a **realistic beginner's budget** for your very first season with **one hive**. You don't need every gadget or upgrade on day one—just the basics to get started safely and effectively.

Starter Budget Breakdown (Per Hive)

Item	What It's For	Estimated Cost (USD)
Hive Kit (Langstroth)	Your bees' home: includes boxes, frames, and foundation	$150 – $250
Bee Package or Nuc	Your starter colony: live bees and a queen	$130 – $200
Protective Suit & Gloves	Keeps you safe during inspections	$80 – $150
Smoker & Hive Tool Kit	Smoker calms bees; tools help open and inspect hives	$30 – $50
Miscellaneous Gear	Bee brush, feeder, entrance reducer, etc.	$20 – $50

Total Estimated Cost: $410 – $700

What's Included & Why You Need It:

Hive Kit ($150–$250):

This is the physical hive where your colony will live. A standard **Langstroth hive** (the most common for beginners) includes:

- **Bottom board** (the hive's foundation)
- **Deep brood boxes** (where the queen lays eggs)
- **Honey supers** (for honey storage and harvesting)
- **Frames and foundation** (where bees build comb)

Some kits even include an inner cover and telescoping lid for weather protection.

Bee Package or Nucleus Colony ($130–$200):

To start your hive, you'll need bees! You can choose from:

- A **3-pound bee package** (around 10,000 bees + a mated queen)
- A **nuc (nucleus colony)**, which includes bees *and* already drawn-out comb on 3–5 frames

Nucs are often slightly more expensive but can grow faster because the bees are already working in a mini hive.

Protective Gear ($80–$150):

Safety first. At minimum, you'll want:

- **A full bee suit** or jacket with veil
- **Gloves** (optional for some, essential for beginners)
  This gear protects you from stings while you're learning to work with bees calmly and confidently.

Smoker & Hive Tools ($30–$50):

A **smoker** emits cool smoke that calms bees during inspections. This reduces stings and makes hive checks smoother.
Your **hive tool** is a multi-use metal bar that pries apart sticky boxes and frames—bees love gluing everything together with propolis!

You'll use these tools every single time you inspect your hive.

Miscellaneous Supplies ($20–$50):

These are small items that really make a difference:

- **Bee brush** – gently moves bees off frames
- **Feeder** – helps provide sugar water in early spring or during drought
- **Entrance reducer** – controls airflow and keeps out robbers (like wasps)

Other Minor Costs to Expect:

- **Sugar** – $10–$20 per month (early feeding support for new colonies)
- **Paint or sealer** – $15–$30 for weatherproofing your hive boxes
- **Mite treatment** – $10–$40 depending on method and necessity
- **Bee journal** – optional, but great for tracking progress

Beginner Tip:

You don't need to **buy everything at once**. Start with the **core essentials** and build from there:

- Buy a solid hive and protective gear first
- Get your bees close to delivery season (spring in most areas)
- Add tools and extras as you gain experience

DIY vs. Pre-Made Equipment

As you prepare to welcome your first bees, one big question may cross your mind: **Should I build my own hive or buy one ready-made?**

The short answer? **Yes, you *can* build your own hive**—especially if you enjoy hands-on projects and have a bit of time and the right tools. In fact, many experienced beekeepers eventually do! But as a beginner, it's important to understand the **pros and cons** before picking up a hammer or clicking "Add to Cart."

Building Your Own Hive (DIY)

Some hive styles—like **Top-Bar** and **Warre hives**—are especially beginner-friendly when it comes to DIY construction. They're simple, use affordable materials like wood planks and screws, and don't require complex joints or power tools. Plans for these can be found online or in beekeeping forums, and customizing them to fit your space can be fun and fulfilling.

DIY Pros:

- **Saves money**: Buying wood and building materials is often cheaper than purchasing a full hive setup.
- **Customizable**: You can modify the size, height, or features to suit your bees or your backyard setup.

- **Hands-on learning**: You'll better understand how the hive works, how parts fit together, and how bees use each section. Great if you're a visual or tactile learner.

DIY Cons:

- **Precision matters**: Bees are surprisingly particular. Gaps that are too large can invite pests; gaps too small may interfere with bee movement or ventilation.
- **Takes time and tools**: If you're short on either, DIY might become more stressful than fun.
- **Not always compatible**: Especially with Langstroth hives, homemade components might not match standard commercial sizes (like frames or foundation), which can limit your options or resale value.

Beginner tip: If you do choose to build, start with a **simple Top-Bar hive** using a reputable plan. Avoid trying to reinvent the wheel—your bees won't appreciate experimental housing.

Buying a Pre-Made Hive

For most beginners, starting with a **pre-assembled or kit-based hive** is the smoothest path. These are typically **Langstroth hives**, which are the most commonly used style in North America. They come in standard sizes, often include all necessary components, and may even arrive **partially assembled or fully built**.

Pre-Made Pros:

- **Beginner-friendly**: No guesswork—just follow the instructions, install your bees, and you're off.
- **Standardized parts**: Easy to replace, upgrade, or expand your system using widely available components.
- **Reliable resale value**: Commercial-grade equipment is easier to sell or pass on if you decide to upgrade or pause beekeeping.

Pre-Made Cons:

- **More expensive upfront**: You're paying for convenience and manufacturing.
- **Less customization**: You get what's in the box; there's less room for creative design or modification.
- **May need painting or weatherproofing**: Even pre-made hives often require a finishing coat before outdoor use.

So, Which Should You Choose?

If you're comfortable with tools and have time before bee season begins, **DIY can be fun and rewarding**—especially for those with a background in woodworking or a love of tinkering. Many beekeepers find it meaningful to build their bees' home with their own hands.

But if this is your **first time keeping bees**, and you're more focused on learning bee care than construction, **starting with a pre-made hive is the way to go**. It removes the pressure of precision building and lets you focus on what really matters: understanding your bees, managing your colony, and learning to inspect, feed, and care for them through the seasons.

Pro Tip: You can always build your **second** hive once you have experience. Many beekeepers do!

Chapter 4

Getting & Setting Up Your Bees

Bringing Your Colony Home the Right Way

You've chosen your hive, picked the perfect location, and double-checked your local beekeeping rules. Now comes the most exciting (and nerve-wracking) step yet: **getting your bees** and helping them settle into their new home.

This chapter walks you through the different ways to acquire bees, how to spot a healthy source, what makes a good queen, and how to safely install your buzzing newcomers into their hive. By the end, you'll be fully equipped to welcome your colony like a pro—even if it's your very first time.

Package Bees vs. Nucleus Colonies vs. Swarm Capture

Three ways to start your hive—and which one's best for beginners

Before you can become a beekeeper, you need the stars of the show: **the bees themselves**. But how exactly do you *get* a hive full of bees?

There are **three primary ways** beginners can start a colony:

1. Package Bees – *The Beginner's Starter Pack*

This is the most **widely used** and accessible way for new beekeepers to begin.

A **bee package** typically includes:

- **Around 3 pounds of bees** (that's roughly 10,000 worker bees!)
- **A caged queen**, who may be newly mated or unmated
- **A can of sugar syrup** to feed the bees during shipment

These bees come in a screened wooden or plastic box and are shipped in spring. When you install them in your hive, you'll need to place the queen cage inside and allow the bees to gradually accept her.

Advantages of Package Bees:

- **Easy to order online** or from local suppliers in early spring
- Gives you a **clean start**: fewer chances of inheriting pests or diseases from another hive

- Ideal if you're **starting with new equipment** or building your first hive from scratch

Drawbacks:

- The bees come from **different colonies**, so they don't naturally follow the queen—they need time to adjust to her scent and presence
- There's **no brood (eggs or larvae)** yet, which means no young bees or established hive rhythm
- There's a **transition period** where bees may seem unsettled until the queen starts laying and brood is present

Best for: Beginners who want a fresh start and are willing to be patient while the colony stabilizes.

2. Nucleus Colony (Nuc) – *The Jump-Start Option*

A **nucleus colony**, or **"nuc"**, is essentially a **starter hive** that already has everything in motion. You receive a **small hive box** (usually wooden or plastic) that contains:

- A **proven, laying queen**
- **3 to 5 frames** of bees, drawn comb, honey, pollen, and most importantly—**developing brood** (eggs, larvae, pupae)
- **Nurse bees and foragers** already working as a team

Because the bees are already settled into their roles and recognize the queen, a nuc gives your beekeeping journey a **head start**.

Advantages of a Nuc:

- Your colony is already **functioning like a mini-hive**—you're plugging into an established rhythm
- No need to wait for the queen to be accepted
- Comes with **drawn comb**, which saves your bees time and energy
- Has a **faster population build-up**, so your hive gains strength quickly

Drawbacks:

- Usually **more expensive** than a package
- Not always available online—most nucs are **sold locally**, and quantities are limited
- Less flexibility: You're working with an **already-set colony structure**, which some purists might see as less "customizable"

Best for: Beginners who want faster results and less risk in early hive development.

3. Swarm Capture – *Nature's Free Bees (But Not for Rookies)*

A **swarm** is a group of bees that has left its original hive—often due to overcrowding—and is looking for a new home. These bees will often cluster on tree branches, fences, or buildings while scout bees search for a permanent location.

Experienced beekeepers sometimes **capture swarms** and rehome them in a hive box.

Advantages of Swarm Capture:

- **Free bees!** (No purchase needed)
- Swarms often have **"survivor stock" genetics**, meaning they may be naturally hardier
- It's a thrilling challenge for skilled beekeepers and helps prevent wild hives from settling in unwanted areas (like someone's attic!)

Drawbacks:

- Requires knowledge, timing, and the **right equipment** (ladders, boxes, veils, etc.)
- No idea what you're getting—**possible disease, mites, or poor genetics**
- Often **illegal** to collect a swarm that may belong to another beekeeper without verification
- Not safe for beginners—you could get stung, drop the swarm, or mishandle the process

Best for: Experienced, confident beekeepers who know how to identify and handle bee behavior.

Package Bees   **Nucleus Colony (Nuc)**   **Swarm Capture**

Which One Should You Choose?

For most beginners, a **nuc** is the easiest and most reliable way to start. It gets your hive off the ground faster and with less uncertainty. However, if nucs aren't available in your area, or if you're working on a tight budget, **package bees** are a perfectly valid—and very common—alternative.

Swarm catching, while romantic and exciting, is best left to your second or third year, after you've gained more experience and confidence handling bees.

Choosing a Healthy Bee Source

One of the **first big decisions** you'll make as a new beekeeper is where to get your bees. And trust us—this isn't something to rush.

Just like you wouldn't adopt a puppy from a sketchy seller, you shouldn't launch your beekeeping journey with unhealthy, poorly bred, or stressed-out bees. The strength, health, and **genetics of your colony** from the very beginning can make or break your entire first season—and potentially your first year.

That's why this section will walk you through:

- Where to buy bees (and where **not** to)
- What to ask before purchasing
- How to spot a healthy colony from the start

Why Bee Source Matters So Much

Bees aren't just bugs in a box—they're **living organisms with complex needs**, behaviors, and risks. Starting with the right colony means you're more likely to:

- Avoid disease outbreaks
- Build a strong, productive hive
- Reduce the chances of colony collapse
- Increase overwintering success
- Enjoy a smoother, more rewarding first season

Choosing well at this stage saves you **time, money, and frustration** later on.

Where to Get Bees – And Why It Matters

Your bees should be:

- **Disease-free**
- **Acclimated to your local environment**
- **Genetically strong with a high-quality queen**

Here are the three most common—and trusted—sources:

1. Local Beekeepers or Breeders (Best Choice)

These are the folks who've raised bees **in your climate**, around your region's plants, pests, and weather patterns. Bees from local sources are more resilient, less stressed during transport, and tend to perform better.

Pros:

- Adapted to local temperatures and seasons
- More resistant to local pests and diseases
- Usually less travel stress (no long-distance shipping)
- Easy to ask questions and get support

2. Local Beekeeping Clubs or Associations

If you're not sure who the local breeders are, **ask your local beekeeping club**. These groups often have vetted supplier lists and sometimes place **group orders**, which can lower your cost and give you access to high-quality bees.

Pros:

- Access to experienced mentors
- Recommendations from seasoned beekeepers
- Group buying discounts and pickups

3. Online Bee Suppliers (Good with Caution)

If you live in an area without local sources, online ordering is a valid option. However, you need to be **extra careful**. Always:

- **Read reviews**
- Check their **health guarantees**
- Make sure they ship **on time** and with **proper ventilation**
- Ask about **queen origin** and disease control

Pro tip: Look for suppliers who offer **locally raised queens** or "northern-bred" bees if you live in cooler climates.

Questions to Ask Before You Buy

To ensure you're getting a healthy, well-bred colony, ask sellers these key questions:

1. **Was the queen bred locally or shipped in from another region?**
   Local queens are better adapted to your climate and environment.
2. **Is the colony free from common diseases and parasites?**
   Especially ask about *Varroa mites*, *American foulbrood*, and *Nosema*.

3. **Have the bees been treated for mites or illness? If so, how?**
   Find out whether treatments were **natural, organic, or synthetic**, and how recently they were applied.
4. **What type of bees are they?** (Italian, Carniolan, Russian, etc.)
   Different breeds have different temperaments and traits. Choose what fits your goals and local conditions.

Pro Tips for Picking the Right Bees

- **Buy bees raised in your climate zone.** Southern-bred bees often struggle in northern winters.
- **Avoid sellers who can't answer questions clearly.** If they dodge or downplay disease risks, that's a red flag.
- **Choose early-season pickups** if possible. This gives your colony more time to build up strength before winter.

Bonus Tip: Why Local is Better Than Cheap

You might find cheaper bee packages online—but beware. **Low cost often means low quality.** Bees raised in bulk, shipped long distances, or produced without care often arrive:

- Weak or queenless
- Overloaded with stress or mites
- Poorly adapted to your area's plants and weather

On the other hand, local bees often:

- Settle into your hive more quickly
- Require fewer treatments
- Are easier to work with (especially for beginners)

And there's one more bonus—**you'll be supporting your local ecosystem and small beekeeping operations.** That's good karma and good beekeeping.

Understanding Queen Bees

When it comes to a honeybee colony, everything revolves around the **queen**. She's not just the biggest bee in the hive—she's the most important. Her presence (or absence) can make or break your beekeeping experience.

Think of her as the **engine of your hive**. She sets the pace for population growth, keeps the colony unified, and directly affects the overall behavior, productivity, and survival of the bees. Without a **strong, healthy queen**, even the most well-placed hive and best equipment won't lead to success.

Why a Good Queen Matters

A healthy queen isn't just "nice to have"—she's essential. Here's why:

- **She lays up to 2,000 eggs a day** in peak season. That's how the hive grows and stays strong.
- **Her pheromones act like hive glue**, keeping worker bees calm, focused, and organized.
- She sets the tone: **good queens mean gentle bees**, steady brood patterns, and full frames of honey.
- A **weak or aging queen** can lead to problems like:
  - **Swarming** (when the colony leaves to find a new home)
  - **Aggression** (more stinging, buzzing, and defensive behavior)
  - **Colony collapse** (when the population dwindles or dies out)

In short: when your queen thrives, your bees thrive.

What to Look for in a Quality Queen

When purchasing or inspecting your queen, here are the must-knows for beginners:

Mated, Not Virgin:

A **mated queen** has already flown out, successfully mated with drones, and is ready to start laying eggs. This is exactly what you want.

A **virgin queen** still needs to go on her mating flight. That means:

- Delay in egg-laying (up to several days or more)
- Risk of never returning (due to weather, predators, or disorientation)
- Potential failure to produce viable brood

Pro tip: If you're just starting out, always begin with a **mated queen** from a trusted breeder or supplier.

Marked Queen:

Most professional queen breeders mark their queens with a **tiny colored dot** on her back. It doesn't hurt her and makes her **so much easier to spot** among thousands of workers.

The color also indicates the year she was born:

- White, yellow, red, green, and blue are used in a rotating 5-year cycle.
- This helps you **track her age** and know when it might be time for a replacement.

Calm Hive Behavior:

When a queen is accepted and doing her job, the hive has a peaceful hum, and the bees move in sync.

But when she's new or hasn't been accepted yet, you might notice:

- Loud buzzing or restlessness
- Bees clustering tightly around her
- A bit of chaos inside the hive

This isn't always bad! **Be patient**. Workers can take a few days to accept a new queen, especially if she was introduced by a beekeeper.

A close-up photo of a marked queen bee on a honeycomb, surrounded by workers

Be Patient: Queens Need Time

When introducing a new queen—whether she's been shipped, bought locally, or raised in your own apiary—understand that **adjustment takes time**. She won't start laying eggs immediately, and the colony might act uneasy for a few days.

This is completely normal. Here's what to do:

- Wait at least **3–5 days** before checking if she's laying
- Resist the urge to disturb the hive too much early on
- Watch for signs like **egg-laying, worker calmness, and even brood pattern** within a week

If there's still no sign of eggs after a full week, **then** you may need to investigate further. But in most cases, a little patience goes a long way.

Setting Up Your Bees Safely

Installing your bees is one of the most unforgettable moments in your beekeeping journey. It's thrilling—yes. But it can also be a little intimidating, especially if it's your first time handling thousands of buzzing insects.

Whether you've received a **package of bees** (typically 3 lbs of bees plus a caged queen) or a **nucleus colony (nuc)** (a small starter hive with frames, bees, brood, and an active queen), this guide will walk you through how to set them up **safely, smoothly**, and **confidently**.

Your job is to make their transition to their new home as **stress-free** as possible—for them and for you.

1. Suit Up Properly

Even if you're a calm, steady soul, remember—your bees are **being moved from their home**, handled, and exposed to a new environment. Even gentle bees can get agitated under stress.

Here's the minimum protective gear you should wear during installation:

- **Full beekeeping suit or jacket**: Protects your arms, legs, and torso
- **Secure veil**: **Always** cover your face and neck—bees are naturally drawn to the face when they feel threatened
- **Gloves**: Especially important if you're new. Once you're more experienced, you can go gloveless if you prefer.

Wearing the right gear doesn't just protect you—it also gives you the confidence to stay calm and focused.

2. Prep the Hive Before Opening the Box

This is a crucial step—and often overlooked by eager beginners!

Before you even bring the bees outside, your hive should be:

- **Set up completely** in its permanent location (don't move it later!)

- **Leveled** front-to-back and side-to-side, so combs hang straight
- **All parts in place**: bottom board, brood box, frames, feeder (if used), inner cover, and lid
- **Clean and dry**—never install bees into a wet hive
- **Feeder filled with 1:1 sugar syrup** if your bees will need supplemental food in their first days (very common for packages)

This preparation allows you to work quickly and confidently once the bees are out of their box.

3. Calm the Bees (Gently—Without Smoke)

You may have seen old-school beekeepers puffing clouds of smoke into their hives. Smoke *does* reduce defensive behavior—but it can also add unnecessary stress, especially for newly transported bees.

Instead, use a **fine mist of 1:1 sugar water** (equal parts sugar and water) sprayed gently over the cluster of bees. This technique:

- **Encourages grooming**, keeping them focused on cleaning themselves
- **Distracts them from flying** during installation
- **Keeps their mood calmer** without overwhelming their senses like smoke might

Tip: Only mist lightly—don't drench the bees. You want them busy, not sticky.

Smoke can still be used sparingly if absolutely needed—but for package bees especially, it's usually best to skip it.

4. Choose the Right Time to Install

When it comes to bee installation, **timing really matters**.

Avoid installing bees if it's:

- Windy
- Raining
- Cold (below **50°F / 10°C**)
- Blazing hot at midday (especially for packages)

Best Time to Install:

A **calm, dry, late afternoon or early evening**. Bees are less likely to fly during this time and are more likely to settle quietly into their hive for the night.

This timing gives them the entire night to **orient themselves, clean the hive, and cluster around the queen** without immediate pressure to forage or defend the entrance.

5. Move Slowly and Stay Calm

Bees don't read your emotions—but they do respond to your **energy**. Sudden, jerky movements or loud noises can feel like a threat.

When installing your bees:

- Use **slow, fluid movements**
- Breathe normally (don't hold your breath or panic)
- Avoid bumping the hive or dropping frames
- Speak softly (if at all)

The goal is to **blend into the environment**, not announce yourself like a clumsy bear.

If a few bees start to buzz around you—it's okay. **Stay still, let them pass, and continue calmly.** Most new beekeepers are surprised at how **peaceful** the installation process feels when done right.

Introducing the Queen

For Package Bees - Helping your hive accept their new ruler

When you install a package of bees, you're not just giving them a new home—you're also giving them a new queen. But bees don't automatically accept a queen they've never met. She needs to be introduced **gradually** so her pheromones (her unique scent that keeps the colony bonded and calm) can spread through the hive.

That's where the **queen cage** and the **candy plug** come in.

Your queen will arrive in a small wooden or plastic cage with a few attendant bees inside and one end blocked by a soft sugar candy. This candy acts as a **time-release mechanism**. As the bees eat through it over a few days, they slowly adjust to her scent— and by the time she's free, she's one of them.

Step-by-Step: Installing the Queen Cage

Follow these simple steps to install the queen cage properly:

1. Remove a few center frames

Open your hive and gently take out 2–3 frames from the center of the brood box. This gives you room to insert the queen cage and makes it easier to pour in the bees.

2. Insert the queen cage (candy end up!)

Wedge the cage between two frames vertically, with the **candy side pointing upward**. This ensures that if a worker dies inside, she doesn't block the exit. Make sure the mesh side of the cage is exposed so bees can make contact with the queen.

3. Add the rest of the bees

Shake the package gently over the hive so the bees fall into the box. Don't worry—it's normal for some to fly around. Alternatively, you can set the open package next to the hive and let them walk in naturally.

4. Close the hive and feed

Replace the lid, and immediately set up a feeder filled with **1:1 sugar syrup** (equal parts sugar and water). Your bees will need this as their main food source for the first few days while they get established.

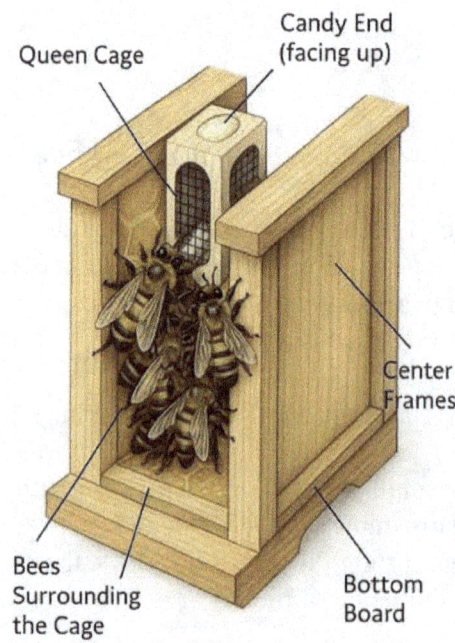

A labeled illustration showing a queen cage inserted between two center frames in a hive, with the candy end facing up and bees around it.

Aftercare: Check for Queen Release

Wait about **3 to 5 days**, then open the hive and check if the queen has been released. Here's what to do:

- If the cage is **empty**—great! She's out and (hopefully) accepted.
- If she's **still inside**, gently remove the candy plug yourself using a small twig or nail, and carefully place the cage back in for her to exit naturally.
- If the queen is **dead or missing**, you'll need to **order a replacement queen immediately**—a hive without a queen cannot survive long.

Troubleshooting Early Problems

Even with the best setup, new hives can hit a few bumps in the beginning. Here's how to spot and solve the most common issues:

Queen Not Released or Missing:

- Check within **3–5 days**
- If the candy wasn't chewed, manually remove it
- If the queen is gone or dead, re-queen ASAP

Bees Leaving the Hive (Absconding):

Sometimes bees will leave a brand-new hive entirely—this is called **absconding**, and it's usually caused by:

- The hive being too hot, exposed, or unstable
- Lack of food or water
- Too much disturbance early on

Prevention Tips:

- Place your hive in a calm, **wind-protected spot**
- Keep syrup feeders full
- **Avoid peeking** inside too often in the first week

Dead Bees at the Entrance:

Don't panic—some bee loss is normal during transport. You may see a small pile at the entrance.

What to do:

- Gently remove the dead bees with a stick or brush
- Wait **24–48 hours** to allow the colony to recover and orient itself

No Brood After 7–10 Days:

If you open your hive after a week and don't see any eggs, larvae, or capped brood, your queen may not be laying—or might be missing entirely.

Check for:

- Tiny white eggs at the bottom of cells
- Jelly-like larvae
- Flat, waxy caps (indicating developing brood)

No signs at all? It may be time to **re-queen the hive**.

Wrapping up…

Congratulations—once your bees are in and your queen is accepted, you've officially created a living, functioning colony. It's no longer just a box of bees… it's a **super-organism** with purpose, energy, and future honey in the making.

But now's not the time to hover. In fact, for the first week, **leave them be** (pun intended). Let your bees settle in, build comb, and let the queen start laying. Constant disturbances can disrupt her rhythm and stress the colony.

Chapter 5

Year-Round Hive Management

Keeping Your Bees Healthy Every Month of the Year

Now that your bees are buzzing and your queen is laying, it's time to zoom out and look at the **big picture**: how to manage your hive through the seasons.

Beekeeping isn't a "set it and forget it" hobby. Bees change with the weather, the blooms, and the temperature. What they need in March is very different from what they need in October. This chapter walks you through a **month-by-month plan** to keep your colony strong, productive, and prepared for the unexpected.

Your first year as a beekeeper is less about buckets of honey and more about building a **strong, healthy foundation** for your hive. It's a season of learning, experimenting, and gaining confidence. Don't expect perfection—expect **progress**.

Your First Year Overview: What to Expect

Your first year as a beekeeper is less about buckets of honey and more about building a **strong, healthy foundation** for your hive. It's a season of learning, experimenting, and gaining confidence. Don't expect perfection—expect **progress**.

Your main goal is simple:

Help your bees grow into a thriving colony that can make it through their first winter.

If honey happens? That's a bonus.

What You'll Be Doing Regularly:

Expect to…

- Inspect the hive every **7–14 days** during spring and summer
- Monitor for **pests**, **queen health**, and **brood patterns**
- Provide **supplemental feeding** when natural nectar is low
- Take notes after every inspection to track progress and problems
- Stay **flexible and observant**—every colony is different

And most importantly—don't panic if things don't go perfectly. Bees have survived for **millions of years**. Your job is to **support, not control** them. Trust their instincts, and stay curious.

Spring (March–May): Growth, Swarms & Foundations

Spring is the official kickoff of the beekeeping year. The queen starts laying eggs again after a quiet winter, and the workers ramp up foraging as flowers begin to bloom. The colony's population **explodes** during this time, and you'll be busy keeping up.

Key Tasks:

Inspect Every 7–10 Days

- Look for **a healthy laying queen** (eggs, larvae, and capped brood)
- Watch for **even, solid brood patterns**—patchy ones may signal a problem
- Make sure the colony has **enough space** for expansion

A clear photo of a healthy brood frame showing eggs, larvae, and capped brood.

Feed If Nectar Is Scarce

- If flowers are still sparse or your colony is newly installed, feed **1:1 sugar syrup** (1 part sugar, 1 part water)
- Use a feeder placed **inside** the hive to prevent robbing

Add Boxes (Supering)

- Once bees have built comb and filled **7+ frames** in the lower box, add a **super** to give them more room
- Too little space = congestion = risk of swarming

Watch for Swarm Signs

- Swarming is how bees reproduce, but you don't want to lose half your colony
- Check for **swarm cells** (large peanut-shaped queen cells, usually on the bottom of frames)
- If needed, perform a **split**—dividing your hive to manage space and prevent swarming

Monitor Spring Weather

- Sudden cold snaps in early spring can stress bees
- Make sure they still have access to **stored honey or syrup** if it's too cold to forage

Summer (June–August): Honey Flow, Heat & Hive Health

Summer is the busiest time for both you and your bees. Flowers are blooming, nectar is flowing, and your hive is **at peak activity**. But this is also when challenges like **overheating, pests, and robbing** become serious threats.

Key Tasks:

Ventilate the Hive

- Hot, humid hives lead to **moisture problems and poor honey curing**
- Use ventilation shims or prop open the **inner cover slightly** to allow air to circulate

Monitor for Pests

- Summer is prime time for **Varroa mites, small hive beetles,** and **wax moths**
- Use methods like:
  - **Sticky boards** (placed under screened bottom boards)
  - **Powdered sugar shake**
  - **Alcohol wash** (more accurate but more invasive)

If Varroa counts are high, begin treatment immediately—these mites are the #1 cause of colony collapse.

Harvest Honey (If Ready)

- Only harvest **capped honey** (cells sealed with white wax)—this means the moisture content is low enough to store safely
- Leave **at least 30–40 pounds** of honey for the bees to use through fall and winter (they need it!)

Capped Cells –
Ready to Harvest

Uncapped Cells
Not Ready

A top-down photo showing capped vs. uncapped honeycomb. Label the capped cells to show what's ready to harvest.

Provide Clean Water

- Bees need **a lot of water** in summer to cool the hive and dilute honey
- Use a shallow tray with:
    - Clean water
    - Pebbles or corks for landing spots
    - Change it every few days to keep it fresh

Prevent Robbing

- In summer droughts, bees from stronger hives may raid weaker ones
- Signs of robbing include:
    - Fighting at the hive entrance
    - Torn wax near honey cells

o Sudden loss of bee population
- Use **entrance reducers** if you suspect robbing, and don't leave sugar syrup or exposed honey near your apiary

Pro Tips for Year One Success:

- Keep a **beekeeping journal**—write down what you saw and did at every inspection
- Take **photos** during inspections for later reference
- Learn from **mistakes**—every beekeeper has made them
- Ask for advice from local **beekeeping associations** or mentors
- Don't rush into harvesting—**a strong, surviving colony** is far more valuable than a few early jars of honey

Fall (September–November): Preparing for Winter

As the leaves turn gold and the air gets crisper, your hive begins to wind down. The colony knows what's coming—and so should you. Fall is a crucial season in beekeeping, not because there's a lot to *do*, but because what you do now determines whether your bees survive the cold months ahead.

You'll notice your **colony shrinking in size**. The queen naturally lays fewer eggs, drones are kicked out (sorry boys), and the workers are focused on **storing food and insulating the hive**. This is a transition season where your role shifts from hands-on to more observational and supportive.

Key Tasks:

Final Mite Treatments

By late summer and early fall, **Varroa mite populations spike**—and that's bad news for overwintering bees. These mites weaken your bees' immune systems, making them more vulnerable to disease and cold stress.

You can use either **natural treatments** (like oxalic acid, formic acid, or essential oils) or **synthetic treatments** (like Apivar). Always read the labels and follow temperature requirements—some treatments can harm bees if applied in cold weather.

Why it matters: Winter bees live longer than summer bees. Keeping them healthy in fall means your hive starts winter with its strongest team.

Consolidate the Hive

As the colony shrinks, they no longer need multiple boxes to move around. In fact, **too much empty space becomes a burden**—it's harder for the cluster to stay warm, and pests have more room to hide.

- **Remove unused honey supers**
- **Reduce the brood chamber** to just one or two boxes
- **Center the frames** with brood and food stores together

Think of this as downsizing for winter efficiency.

Feed if Honey Stores Are Low

Check how much honey is in the hive. Your bees need **at least 60–90 pounds of stored honey** to survive the winter, depending on your climate.

If they're light on stores:

- Feed **2:1 sugar syrup** (2 parts sugar to 1 part water)
- Add feeders inside the hive (frame or top feeders work well)
- Stop feeding once temperatures drop too low (syrup can ferment or freeze)

Tip: Feeding early allows bees time to convert syrup into storable honey before it gets too cold.

Install Mouse Guards

As nights get colder, mice begin looking for warm places—and a beehive full of food and insulation is basically a rodent palace.

Install **mouse guards** at the hive entrance:

- Metal or plastic mesh that lets bees through but blocks rodents
- Available at most beekeeping supply stores
- Keeps out voles and other small intruders too

Block Wind & Insulate (for Cold Climates)

If you live in an area with freezing winters, **wind chill and moisture are your hive's biggest enemies**.

How to help:

- Wrap hives with **breathable hive wraps** (not plastic tarps)
- Use **foam boards** or insulating blankets
- Place a windbreak (like straw bales or fencing) to shield from prevailing wind
- Consider adding a **moisture quilt box** to absorb condensation

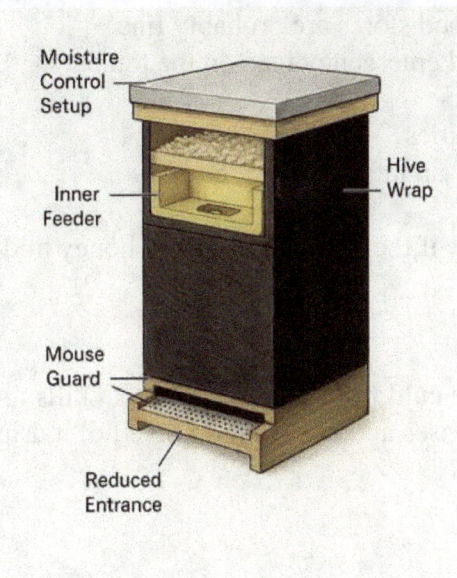

Moisture
Control
Setup

Inner
Feeder

Hive
Wrap

Mouse
Guard

Reduced
Entrance

A clear diagram showing a properly wrapped fall hive, with mouse guard, reduced entrance, inner feeder, and moisture control setup.

Winter (December–February): Survival Mode

Winter is when your hive goes completely quiet—but don't be fooled. Inside, your bees are alive, huddled in a **tight cluster** around the queen, gently vibrating their wings to generate heat.

They don't leave the hive (unless it's above 50°F for a short flight), and you shouldn't disturb them either. This is a season of trust—**you've prepared them, now let nature do the rest**.

Key Tasks:

No Opening the Hive

This can be hard, especially for new beekeepers—but resist the urge to peek inside. Breaking the cluster exposes bees to cold air, which can kill them instantly.

If you must check inside (e.g. for suspected moisture), do it on a warm afternoon and work fast.

Check Hive Weight

Once every 2–3 weeks, do a **"heft test"**—gently lift the back of the hive about an inch.

- If it feels **heavy**, food stores are probably fine
- If it feels **light**, add emergency feed on the top bars:
  - Sugar bricks
  - Fondant patties
  - Dry sugar (mountain camp method)

This may save your colony if they run out of stored honey midwinter.

Moisture Control

Oddly enough, it's **not the cold but condensation** that kills more bees in winter. When warm air from the cluster rises and hits the cold hive lid, it drips down on bees—leading to death by hypothermia.

Prevent this by:

- Using **quilt boxes** filled with wood shavings
- Installing **moisture boards** or absorbent layers
- Tipping the hive slightly forward so moisture runs out the front

Clear the Entrance

Make sure snow, ice, or dead bees don't clog the entrance. Bees need airflow to prevent suffocation and to allow for brief **cleansing flights** on warm days.

Pro Tip:

If you see bees flying in January or February, **they're not confused**—they're relieving themselves after weeks indoors. It's a good sign!

A winter hive cutaway showing bees in cluster, moisture board, sugar brick on top bars, and slightly tipped hive for drainage.

Monthly Maintenance Checklist (Quick Reference)

Month	Key Tasks
March	Inspect hive, feed syrup if light, clean bottom board
April	Check brood pattern, prep for swarm season, add supers
May	Watch for swarms, split hives if needed, manage mites
June	Add water source, manage heat, start honey harvest
July	Continue harvesting, test for mites, prevent robbing
August	Begin mite treatment, reduce entrances, evaluate stores
September	Feed 2:1 syrup, final mite treatment, install mouse guards
October	Wrap hive (cold climates), remove unused boxes
November	Stop inspections, check insulation, add moisture control
Dec–Feb	Do NOT open hive, monitor weight, add sugar bricks if light

Wrapping up…

Successful beekeeping isn't about reacting day by day—it's about thinking **in rhythm with nature**. Your hive doesn't operate on your calendar; it follows the sun, the temperature, and the flowering cycle of plants.

By learning to **plan seasonally**, you'll become more than a beekeeper—you'll become a thoughtful, responsive caretaker. You'll anticipate what your bees need *before* they show signs of stress. You'll work smarter, not harder. And most importantly, your bees will thrive.

In the next chapter, we'll take a deeper look at **the tools and equipment you'll need**, how to choose wisely without overspending, and how to set up your hive for long-term success.

Chapter 6

Preventing Disease, Pests & Colony Collapse

Keeping your hive healthy, resilient, and thriving

Now that you've built your hive, welcomed your bees, and learned the rhythms of the seasons, it's time to talk about what can go wrong—and how to stop it.

Bee colonies are delicate ecosystems. They thrive when balanced, but that balance can tip quickly due to pests, pathogens, poor nutrition, or environmental stress. While this chapter might sound like the "scary" part of beekeeping, don't worry—we're not here to overwhelm you. We're here to **equip you** with the confidence to spot trouble early, act decisively, and keep your colony buzzing with life.

Let's look at the most common threats, how to spot them, and how to fight back— naturally, responsibly, and effectively.

Common Pests

Your hive is warm, full of food, and crowded with life. Naturally, it attracts a few unwanted visitors. Some are just nuisances. Others, if ignored, can be **fatal**.

Let's meet the usual suspects.

1. Varroa Mites (*Varroa destructor*)

The single biggest threat to honeybees worldwide. These reddish-brown mites latch onto adult bees and larvae, feeding on their fat stores (not blood, as once believed). They also transmit a deadly cocktail of viruses that weaken bees from the inside out.

A small mite problem becomes a big one **fast**—especially in late summer or fall. If not treated, the colony can **collapse within weeks**.

Signs:

- **Deformed wings** (a sign of Deformed Wing Virus)
- **Trembling, disoriented bees** at the hive entrance
- **Patchy or irregular brood pattern**
- **Visible mites** on adult bees or drone brood

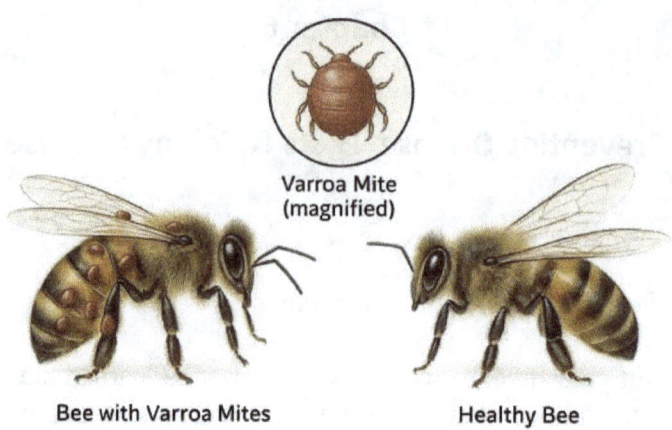

Varroa Mite
(magnified)

Bee with Varroa Mites   Healthy Bee

Side-by-side photo of a bee with visible varroa mites vs. a healthy bee, plus magnified inset of a mite.

2. Small Hive Beetles

These beetles are small but destructive. Adult beetles enter the hive and lay eggs in cracks and corners. When larvae hatch, they **tunnel through comb**, contaminating honey and pollen.

Signs:

- **Slimy comb and a rotten or fermented smell** (from beetle larvae feces)
- **Shiny black beetles** crawling on the inner cover or frames
- **Sunken, greasy-looking honeycomb**

Beetles thrive in warm, humid environments—southern regions should be especially vigilant.

3. Wax Moths

More of a cleanup crew than a predator, wax moths lay eggs in hives that are weak or abandoned. Their larvae eat old comb, leaving behind webbing and destruction.

Strong hives **usually fight them off**, but weak or poorly managed ones are vulnerable.

Signs:

- **Webbing** in corners or frames
- **Silken tunnels** running through the comb
- **Cocoons** lodged in wood crevices

Tip: If your hive is healthy and active, wax moths won't be a problem. They only attack when bees can't defend themselves.

4. Ants, Wasps & Rodents

These freeloaders don't usually destroy the hive—but they **steal resources and stress out your bees**.

- **Ants** go after spilled sugar or honey.
- **Wasps** raid hives for brood or nectar—especially in summer/fall.
- **Mice** sneak in during winter and nest inside warm hives, chewing through comb and insulation.

Prevention Tips:

- Elevate the hive
- Use ant moats or cinnamon barriers
- Reduce entrances during wasp season
- Install mouse guards in fall

Bee Diseases

Pests like mites and beetles are easy to spot with the naked eye. But **diseases?** Not so much. They're sneaky—and they show up in subtle ways that only a watchful beekeeper will notice.

Learning to "read the frames" in your hive—especially in the brood nest—is one of the **most powerful skills** you can develop. It's like understanding your bees' language when something isn't right.

Let's walk through the **most common diseases** you may encounter, how to recognize them, and what actions to take.

1. American Foulbrood (AFB)

The most destructive brood disease—and a nightmare scenario.

AFB is a **bacterial disease** that infects bee larvae inside capped brood cells. The bacteria produce **spores** that are nearly indestructible. They can survive for decades in woodenware, wax, and tools. If it strikes your hive, it's often a **total loss**.

What to Look For:

- **Sunken, greasy, or perforated cappings** on brood cells (healthy cappings are dry and slightly domed)
- **Larvae that look melted or gooey**, turning brown and decomposing inside the cell
- **Ropy test**: Insert a toothpick into the dead larva, stir, and pull up—**if it stretches like slime**, AFB is likely present

- **Sour or foul odor** coming from the brood area

What to Do:

- AFB is a **reportable disease** in most countries
- Infected colonies must often be **burned completely**, including the hive box and frames
- **Never reuse** any equipment from an AFB-positive colony

AFB is extremely contagious. Early detection is critical for protecting your entire apiary—and your neighbor's too.

2. European Foulbrood (EFB)

Less severe than AFB—but still serious, especially in stressed or hungry colonies.

EFB is also caused by bacteria but behaves differently than AFB. It often pops up in **early spring** or when the colony is under stress (cold snaps, poor nutrition, overcrowding).

What to Look For:

- **Twisted, yellowish larvae** lying in uncapped brood cells (they may appear dehydrated or contorted)
- **Watery larval remains** that look like they've collapsed in on themselves
- **Spotty brood pattern**, with empty cells in between healthy ones
- A **mild sour smell** (not as strong as AFB)

What to Do:

- EFB can sometimes be treated with **antibiotics**, but this depends on local laws
- **Requeening** with a more hygienic queen strain can help
- **Feeding and reducing stress** may allow bees to overcome the infection naturally

3. Nosema

A gut parasite that thrives in long winters and damp hives.

Nosema isn't a brood disease—it affects **adult bees**, especially in the early spring or late winter when bees are confined inside and can't take cleansing flights.

There are two main species (Nosema apis and Nosema ceranae), both of which infect the bee's digestive system.

What to Look For:

- **Brown streaks or spots at the hive entrance** or on frames (bee diarrhea)
- **Bees crawling near the hive**, unable to fly
- A general drop in colony strength, productivity, and **queen performance**
- Weak buildup in spring, or unexplained absences of foragers

What to Do:

- Improve **ventilation** inside the hive to reduce moisture
- Replace old comb regularly
- Feed sugar syrup with probiotics or supplements (like Fumidil B, if allowed)
- In mild cases, colonies **recover naturally** with proper care

4. Chalkbrood & Sacbrood (Viral and Fungal Infections)

These diseases kill larvae before they can pupate. Often weather-related.

Both chalkbrood and sacbrood cause **larval death** and are often linked to **excess moisture, poor airflow**, or **genetics** (some queen lines are more prone).

Signs of Chalkbrood:

- **White or gray "mummified" larvae** in brood cells or at the bottom of the hive
- **Dead larvae** look dry and chalky
- **Spotty brood patterns**, with visible gaps and mixed-aged brood

Signs of Sacbrood:

- **Larvae die inside the cell**, turning yellowish or grey
- Appear **fluid-filled** or stretched like a "sack"
- Remain curled in a C-shape and often dry into a brittle scale

What to Do:

- Improve **airflow and reduce humidity** in the hive
- Requeen with a **disease-resistant strain**
- Clean and rotate comb more frequently
- Usually resolves on its own with environmental correction

Monitoring Techniques

In beekeeping, **what you don't see can hurt you.** Many pests and diseases start quietly, building up in the background until one day… boom—your hive is crashing, your bees are dying, and honey production has stopped cold.

That's why **monitoring is everything**. The secret to healthy hives isn't waiting for problems to show up—it's spotting tiny issues *before* they become big ones. And the good news? It's not hard. You just need the right techniques, consistency, and a little time.

Let's walk through exactly how to do it.

Regular Hive Inspections

Your first and best line of defense is simply **opening your hive and looking inside**. Not every day—but on a smart, seasonal schedule.

How Often to Inspect

- **Spring & Summer:** Every **7–10 days** (peak season—bees are building fast, so issues escalate quickly)
- **Fall:** Every **2–3 weeks**
- **Winter:** Leave them alone unless there's a serious concern (cold air can harm the cluster)

What to Look For During Inspections

1. Healthy Brood Pattern

    - A strong queen lays in a tight, consistent pattern.
    - You want to see **solid patches of eggs, larvae, and capped brood**, not scattered or spotty ones.

2. Fresh Eggs

    - Seeing tiny rice-shaped eggs in the cells? Great. That means the queen is present and laying within the last 3 days.

3. No Foul Smell

    - Healthy hives smell sweet and earthy.
    - A rotten or sour smell may signal **American Foulbrood (AFB)** or other dangerous infections.

4. No Uninvited Guests

    - Watch for **varroa mites** on bees' backs or larvae.
    - Also check for **small hive beetles**, **wax moths**, or weird larvae in comb corners.

Keep a Hive Journal

Record what you observe at every visit:

- Date of inspection
- Hive behavior
- Queen status
- Brood condition
- Honey/pollen stores
- Any pests or anomalies

Why it matters: Subtle changes over time are often more important than what you see in a single visit. Your journal helps you detect patterns, prevent surprises, and document treatments.

Mite Monitoring: Varroa Counts

Let's talk about the elephant in the hive: **Varroa destructor**, the parasitic mite responsible for most colony collapses. Even strong hives can fall to them if left unchecked.

And here's the truth: **you can't just eyeball mite levels.** Even a seemingly "healthy" hive might be crawling with invisible trouble.

To know for sure, you need to test.

Two Reliable Monitoring Methods:

1. The Sugar Roll Test *(Non-lethal)*

A safe, bee-friendly way to estimate mite loads.

Steps:

- Collect about **300 bees** (about half a cup) from the brood nest into a jar with a mesh lid.
- Add 2 tablespoons of **powdered sugar**, seal the lid, and gently roll the jar to coat the bees.
- After a few minutes, shake the jar over a white sheet or bowl. The sugar dislodges the mites, which fall through the mesh.
- Count the mites, then release the bees back into the hive.

Threshold:

- **9+ mites per 300 bees** = Time to treat.

Pros: Bees survive, simple to do at home.
Tip: Do this during warm, dry days—sugar clumps in humidity.

2. The Alcohol Wash Test *(More accurate, but lethal)*

A precise method used by commercial and advanced beekeepers.

Steps:

- Collect 300 bees as before.
- Place them in a jar with rubbing alcohol.
- Shake to dislodge the mites.
- Strain and count the mites in the liquid.

Threshold:

- If mite levels are over **3% (i.e., 9 mites per 300 bees)**, immediate treatment is necessary.

Pros: Extremely accurate
Cons: Bees die during testing. Use sparingly and with purpose.

When You Spot a Problem

Even with perfect care, issues will arise. That's normal. What sets good beekeepers apart is **how quickly and calmly they respond**.

Common threats:

- **Varroa mites** (manage aggressively)
- **Nosema** (fungal infection; treat with proper nutrition and ventilation)
- **American Foulbrood** (deadly bacterial disease—requires destruction of infected frames in most regions)
- **Small Hive Beetles** (trap and control with hive management)

Don't panic. You're not alone. Beekeepers around the world face these exact same challenges. With early detection and proper tools, most issues are manageable—and many are reversible.

Natural Treatments vs. Chemical Interventions

When it comes to keeping your bees healthy and protecting them from pests and diseases (like varroa mites, nosema, or foulbrood), you'll generally have **two main options**:

1. **Natural (or organic) treatments**
2. **Chemical (synthetic) interventions**

Both methods are commonly used in modern beekeeping—and both have their pros, cons, and ideal use cases. The key is understanding **when and how** to apply each approach in a way that protects both your bees *and* your honey.

Let's break it down:

Natural (Organic) Treatments

Natural treatments are typically derived from **plant-based oils, organic acids**, or **management strategies** that work with the bees' natural behavior. Many of these are accepted in **organic beekeeping programs**.

Pros:

- Safer for the bees when used properly
- Leaves little to no chemical residue in wax or honey
- Sustainable and accepted in organic operations
- Can be repeated more frequently with fewer side effects

Cons:

- Sometimes less potent for severe infestations
- Can be temperature-sensitive or require precise timing
- May need more consistent monitoring

Examples include:

Oxalic Acid (dribble or vaporization)

- **Best for:** Late fall or winter, when hives are broodless
- **How it works:** Kills exposed mites on adult bees
- **Note:** Safe for bees if dosed correctly. Must wear protective gear when handling.
- **Effectiveness:** Very high during broodless periods
- **Caution:** Won't kill mites hiding inside brood cells

Formic Acid (Formic Pro or MiteAway Quick Strips)

- **Best for:** Spring through fall
- **How it works:** Penetrates capped brood cells to kill mites where they reproduce
- **Pros:** One of the few treatments that kills mites inside brood
- **Cons:** Can be harsh in hot weather; follow temperature guidelines strictly

Essential Oils (Thymol, Lemongrass, Eucalyptus)

- **Best for:** Preventative or mild infestations
- **How it works:** Disrupts mite behavior and reproduction
- **Effectiveness:** Moderate; often used as part of an integrated strategy
- **Pro Tip:** Use in well-ventilated hives and follow product instructions

Screened Bottom Boards

- **What it is:** A ventilated hive floor that allows mites to fall through
- **Best for:** Year-round passive control
- **Effectiveness:** Low on its own, but good for reducing mite loads when combined with other methods

Hive Splits / Brood Breaks

- **How it works:** Temporarily disrupts the bee brood cycle, which interrupts mite reproduction
- **Best for:** Spring or summer management
- **Why it works:** Mites need brood to reproduce. No brood = fewer mites.
- **Bonus:** Also a great way to expand your apiary with new colonies

Chemical (Synthetic) Interventions:

These are lab-formulated products designed specifically to kill mites or treat disease. They're powerful tools—but require **strict adherence** to usage guidelines to protect your bees and avoid resistance.

Pros:

- Often stronger and faster-acting
- Useful for **emergency situations** when natural options aren't working
- Can bring colonies back from the brink

Cons:

- May leave **chemical residues** in honey or wax
- Overuse can lead to **resistance** in pests like varroa mites
- Not compatible with organic beekeeping
- Requires careful handling and strict adherence to dosage and timing

Examples include:

Apivar (Amitraz Strips)

- **Best for:** Varroa control during active brood cycles
- **How it works:** Slow-release miticide absorbed through bee contact
- **Effectiveness:** Very high—often the go-to choice for severe mite problems
- **Caution:** Must be removed before honey supers are added

CheckMite + (Coumaphos), Apistan (Fluvalinate)

- **Older treatments** once widely used
- **Why caution is needed:** Mites in many regions have developed **resistance**
- **Use sparingly,** and never back-to-back seasons

Antibiotics (Oxytetracycline, Tylosin)

- **Only for:** Diagnosed cases of European Foulbrood (EFB) or other bacterial diseases
- **Important:** Only use under **veterinary guidance** and with a proper diagnosis
- **Reminder:** Improper use can lead to resistance and honey contamination

So... Which Should You Use?

There's no one-size-fits-all answer. The **right approach depends on several factors**, such as:

- **Your personal philosophy** (natural vs. conventional)
- **The severity of the issue** (preventative or emergency treatment?)
- **Time of year** (some treatments aren't safe during honey flow)
- **Hive strength and population**
- **Local climate and temperature** (some treatments are temperature-sensitive)
- **Your long-term beekeeping goals** (hobby vs. production)

Rotate Your Treatments

Important Note:

Never rely on **just one method** year after year. Parasites and pathogens are smart—they adapt quickly. The key to long-term success is **rotating treatments** and **monitoring mite levels** regularly (more on that in later chapters).

By using a variety of approaches, you:

- Reduce resistance development
- Minimize chemical buildup in wax or honey
- Protect your bees' long-term health

Boosting Colony Immunity

If you'd rather avoid medicating your bees and reduce the risk of disease altogether, here's the good news: **a strong colony is often its own best defense**.

Think of your hive like a little bee city. When the infrastructure is solid—clean, well-fed, and well-managed—your bees can defend themselves against many of the common threats like mites, disease, and stress. Just like humans, **prevention is way more effective than treatment**.

Here's how to build up your bees' natural immunity and create an environment that sets them up to thrive:

1. Feed Sugar Syrup & Pollen Patties During Dearths

During nectar or pollen shortages (called **dearths**), bees may struggle to find enough natural food to stay energized and productive.

- **Sugar syrup** (1:1 in spring, 2:1 in fall) gives bees the quick energy they need to forage and maintain brood.
- **Pollen patties** supplement protein to help raise healthy young bees.

When to Feed:

- Early spring before blooms open
- During droughts or extended rainy periods
- In fall when natural forage declines

2. Provide Clean, Nearby Water

Bees **need water every day**—to cool the hive, thin honey, feed larvae, and regulate humidity.

- Place a **shallow water source** (like a plant saucer with pebbles or floating corks) **within 10–20 feet** of your hive.
- Change it every few days to prevent algae or mosquito breeding.

A consistent, clean water supply reduces stress and supports hive health.

3. Keep the Hive Dry & Well Ventilated

Moisture is the enemy of bee health. A damp hive encourages:

- Mold and bacteria
- Nosema and chalkbrood infections
- Chilled brood (baby bees)

Make sure:

- Your hive has a **slight tilt forward** to drain condensation
- There's **top ventilation** or an upper entrance in humid climates
- The hive is raised off the ground to avoid damp soil

4. Avoid Crowding or Stacking Hives Too Close

Too many hives crammed into one area can:

- Spread disease faster
- Increase robbing (bees from one hive stealing from another)

- Confuse returning foragers (drift)

Space hives at least **3 feet apart**. Use **visual markers** (plants, paint, patterns) so bees can identify their home

5. Reduce Unnecessary Inspections

While inspections are crucial for early detection, too much disturbance stresses the colony.

- Over-smoking, frequent opening, or rough handling can interrupt brood care, cause queen rejection, or trigger defensive behavior.

Aim for one **quick, calm inspection every 7–10 days** during active seasons. Use **gentle movements** and **minimal smoke**

6. Use Hygienic Queens

Some queens are bred from **hygienic stock**, meaning their offspring have a stronger instinct to:

- Detect and remove diseased or dead brood
- Reduce the spread of viruses, mites, and bacteria
- Keep the hive cleaner overall

Ask your breeder about **VSH (Varroa-Sensitive Hygiene)** or **hygienic-tested queens**

By following these simple but powerful practices, you'll reduce the chances of disease taking hold and help your colony **stay strong naturally**—with less need for medications or interventions. A resilient colony is a productive one—and a happy beekeeper's dream.

Hive Warning Signs and What to Do About It

Even the healthiest hives can run into trouble. As the beekeeper, it's your job to spot issues **early**, before they grow into full-blown problems. Think of this chapter as your **"bee first aid kit"**—a quick-reference guide to help you decode what your hive is telling you, what it might mean, and how to respond with calm confidence.

Just like people, bees have ways of showing distress. You'll notice it in how they fly (or don't), how their brood looks, how the comb smells, or even how many bees are lying motionless at the entrance. These warning signs don't necessarily mean your colony is doomed—but they **are signals** that something's not right.

Below is your field guide to the most common symptoms, what's probably causing them, and what steps you should take to support your bees.

Hive Health Quick Reference Table

Warning Sign	Possible Causes	What You Should Do
Spotty or Irregular Brood Pattern **(You see scattered, inconsistent larvae or capped brood instead of a tight, uniform pattern)**	- Failing or missing queen - Brood diseases like EFB (European Foulbrood) or AFB (American Foulbrood)	- Look for **fresh eggs or queen cells** (this confirms if the queen is still active) - If **no eggs or queen cells**, it may be time to **re-queen** - If larvae look **twisted, discolored, or smell foul**, isolate the hive and **contact your local beekeeping extension** or inspector
Bees Crawling but Not Flying **(Bees seem confused or grounded)**	- **Pesticide poisoning** - **Nosema** (a gut parasite) - Poor nutrition	- Remove and properly dispose of dead bees - Feed sugar syrup with **probiotic additives or Nosema treatment** if needed - Talk to neighbors about chemical sprays used on nearby lawns or gardens
Excessive Dead Bees at the Entrance **(A carpet of dead bees near the hive opening)**	- Cold snap or sudden weather change - Starvation - Viral infection or toxic exposure	- Check internal food stores—if empty or low, add a **sugar board or syrup feeder** - Ensure the hive is **protected from wind and insulated** in cold months - If deaths are sudden and large-scale, check for **signs of mites or viruses**
Deformed Wings on Emerging Bees **(New bees have crumpled, misshaped wings and weak flight)**	- **Varroa mite infestation** - Deformed Wing Virus (DWV), often transmitted by mites	- Perform a **mite count** using the **sugar roll or alcohol wash method** - Begin **mite treatment immediately** (oxalic acid vaporization, formic acid pads, or other IPM strategies)
Strong Foul Odor or Slimy, Sunken Comb **(Hive smells bad or brood comb looks greasy/slimy)**	- **Small Hive Beetle larvae infestation** - **Foulbrood** infection (either AFB or EFB)	- Carefully **remove infected frames** and **seal them in bags** - **Burn contaminated equipment** if advised - **Isolate the hive** and alert your local apiary inspector

		- Sanitize all hive tools and gloves afterward

What If You're Not Sure?

Don't guess. If something seems wrong but you're unsure what's happening:

1. Take **clear photos and videos** of the brood, bees, and hive interior
2. Reach out to one or more of the following:

   - A **local beekeeping club or mentor**
   - Your **county extension office**
   - A **certified apiary inspector** or bee specialist in your area

Most experienced beekeepers are happy to help, and acting early can save not just your hive—but nearby hives as well.

Observation Is Your Best Tool

Bees don't use words—but they do "talk" through behavior. Your job as a beekeeper is to pay attention:

- Are they flying like normal?
- Is traffic in and out of the hive steady and purposeful?
- Is the brood pattern healthy and tight?
- Does the hive smell sweet and waxy—or odd and sour?

The more time you spend **watching calmly**, the more tuned in you'll become. Over time, you'll develop that elusive sixth sense: you'll just *know* when something's off.

Wrapping up…

Bee diseases and pests can feel intimidating at first—but remember, you're not alone. Bees have been managing pests for millions of years, and modern beekeepers have more tools than ever to support them.

Your job isn't to panic—it's to **observe, record, act when needed, and always learn**.

As you continue your journey, you'll develop a sixth sense for hive health. You'll notice what "normal" looks like—and when something feels off. With each inspection, you're becoming not just a beekeeper, but a **guardian of balance in nature**.

Chapter 7

Harvesting and Processing Honey

From Hive to Jar — the Sweetest Part of Beekeeping

You've nurtured your hive, kept your bees healthy, and watched them work tirelessly. Now comes one of the most rewarding parts of your beekeeping journey—**harvesting honey**.

But here's the truth: while pulling frames full of golden honey is exciting, it must be done **responsibly**. Your bees come first, and your honey harvest is a reward for managing the colony well—not a guarantee. This chapter will guide you through **when and how to harvest**, how to **process your honey safely**, and what you need to know if you decide to **sell your honey legally**.

When and When Not to Harvest

Beekeeping is about balance—yours and theirs.

It's tempting. You open the hive, see frames glistening with golden honey, and think, "Time to taste the sweet rewards!" But hold that jar—because harvesting honey isn't just about what you want. It's about what your **bees** need to survive.

Honey is not just a treat; it's their **food source**. Especially in fall and winter, honey is what keeps the colony alive when flowers are no longer blooming. So before you pull a single frame, you'll want to understand exactly **when it's safe**—and when it's not.

When to Harvest

Only collect honey when these key conditions are met:

The Honey is Fully Capped:

Bees seal (or "cap") cells filled with ripe honey using a thin layer of wax. This means the moisture level is just right and the honey won't ferment or spoil. If you see **uncapped nectar**, it's not ready yet.

The Colony is Strong & Populated:

Check for:

- Plenty of bees covering multiple frames

- Active foraging and pollen coming in
- Healthy brood (eggs, larvae, capped cells)

If the colony is **struggling**, don't add stress by taking their food away.

There's More Than Enough Honey Left:

Even if your frames are bursting with capped honey, you must leave **enough stores** behind:

- **30–60 pounds of honey** for winter, especially in colder regions
- That's roughly **2 full deep frames per hive body**, or **5–6 medium frames**

Capped Honeycomb
Ready to Harvest

Uncapped Honeycomb
Not Ready

A zoomed-in visual showing the difference between sealed (safe to harvest) vs. open nectar cells (not ready)

Do NOT Harvest If:

Be patient. Some seasons are about building, not taking.

It's Early Spring:

In spring, colonies are just rebuilding after winter. They need **every drop** of nectar to raise new brood and expand. Let them gather and grow before taking anything.

Most Frames Are Uncapped:

Even if a frame looks full, if it's not **capped**, the moisture level is too high. Unripe honey can ferment and spoil—wasting all your hard work.

The Colony is Weak or Stressed:

If you notice signs of stress (fewer bees, disease, queenless hives, pests like mites), let the bees keep everything. They need all their energy—and stores—to recover.

It's Late Fall or Winter:

Late-season honey is survival fuel. Removing it could starve your bees. If it's chilly enough for you to wear a sweater, it's too late to harvest.

The Many Types of Honey

Your bees are artists—and every jar is a unique masterpiece.

Honey isn't "just honey." Its **flavor, color, thickness, and aroma** vary depending on what flowers your bees visited. That means every batch you harvest will tell the story of your landscape, your season, and your hive.

Here are some popular (and tasty) varieties:

- **Wildflower Honey** – A medley of local blooms. Color and flavor vary based on what's blooming nearby.
- **Clover Honey** – Very light and sweet. Common in grocery stores and beginner hives.
- **Orange Blossom Honey** – Light golden with floral, citrus notes. Sourced from bees near citrus groves.
- **Buckwheat Honey** – Thick, dark, and strong—like molasses. Packed with antioxidants.
- **Sourwood, Tupelo, Lavender** – Specialty honeys with delicate, often region-specific flavors. Prized for their uniqueness and complexity.

There's even **creamed honey** (smooth, spreadable), **comb honey** (honey still inside wax comb), and **infused honey** (flavored with herbs or spices).

Harvesting Methods: From Hive to Jar

Choose your method based on your hive style, goals, and gear.

Method 1: Crush and Strain

Best for: Small-scale beginners, top-bar hives, first-time harvests

How it works:

1. Cut comb off the frame using a clean knife.
2. Place it in a clean container and crush it using a **potato masher or spoon**.

3. Pour the mashed wax and honey mixture through **cheesecloth or a fine sieve**.
4. Let it sit for 24–48 hours.
5. Bottle the clear honey once it settles.

Pros:

- Inexpensive and easy to do at home
- No special tools required
- Great for rustic or comb honey lovers

Cons:

- You lose the comb (bees must rebuild it)
- More work for the bees = slower next harvest

Method 2: Traditional Extraction

Best for: Langstroth hives, repeat harvesters, people looking to scale

How it works:

1. Remove fully capped frames from the hive.
2. Uncap the wax using a hot knife or uncapping fork.
3. Place frames in a **manual or electric honey extractor** (a spinning drum).
4. Spin to force honey out via centrifugal force.
5. Filter, let settle, then bottle.

Pros:

- Preserves the wax comb (bees reuse it)
- Cleaner, faster, and more efficient
- Ideal for larger harvests

Cons:

- Requires equipment (manual extractors start at ~$100)
- More setup and cleanup time

Manual Honey Extractor

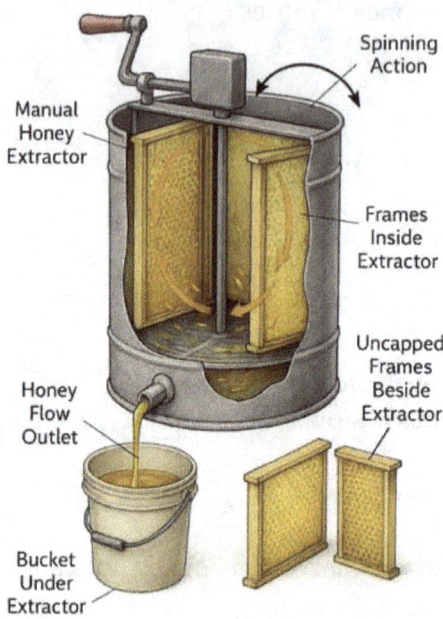

An image of a simple manual honey extractor in use with honey spinning out, bucket underneath, and uncapped frames beside

Method 3: Comb Honey (No Extractor Needed!)

Comb honey is the **purest, most natural form** of honey—just as the bees made it. Instead of extracting liquid honey from the comb, you harvest and serve **whole, sealed sections of honeycomb**, wax and all.

Why It's Popular:

- **Visual Appeal**: Customers love the **beautiful, rustic look** of honey still in the comb. It feels "untouched" and authentic.
- **No Processing Needed**: There's no need for extractors, filters, or spinning machines—just slice and package.
- **Edible Wax**: Beeswax is edible and adds texture, especially when served with cheese, bread, or fruit.

What You'll Need:

- Special **comb honey frames**, **section boxes**, or **Ross Rounds** (round containers placed in the hive).
- A **clean knife** or cutter to separate comb sections once fully capped.

Tip for Beginners: Bees need strong nectar flow and space to draw out perfect comb. Comb honey works best when your colony is thriving and well-managed.

Removing Bees from Honey Supers

Before you harvest honey—comb or liquid—you'll need to remove the bees from the **honey supers** (the top boxes where surplus honey is stored). You want to do this gently so you don't stress the bees or end up with stingers in your sleeves.

Here are three beginner-friendly methods:

1. Bee Escape Board

A **one-way door** for bees.

- Placed between the **brood box** and **honey supers**
- Bees move **down through the board**, but can't come back up
- Leave on for **24–48 hours**, then check if supers are bee-free

Best for: Hobbyists who want **minimal disruption** and don't mind waiting a day or two.

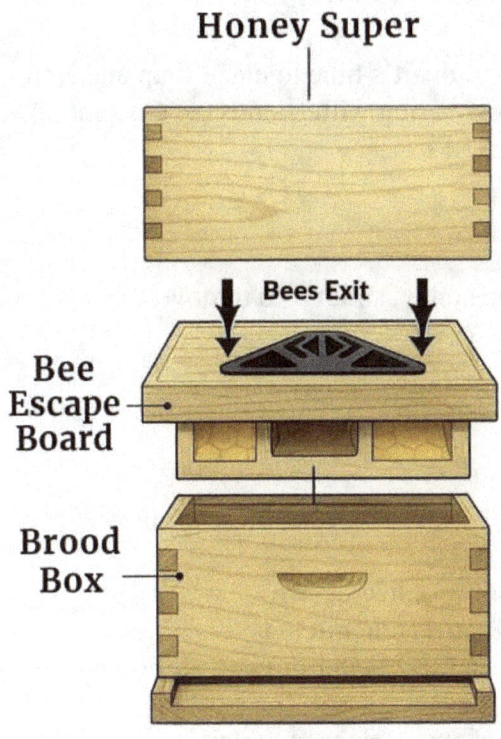

A top-down illustration of a Bee Escape Board Diagram showing how bees move out of the honey super through the board.

2. Fume Board (with Natural Repellents)

This is a **quick method** that uses scent to encourage bees to move away from the honey.

- A fume board is a lid lined with absorbent material
- Apply **natural repellents** like almond oil, thyme oil, or commercial bee-safe sprays
- Place on top of super for **5–10 minutes**—bees will move downward

Pro tip: Use in **warm weather** (heat activates the repellent), and monitor closely to avoid overheating or stressing the colony.

3. Manual Brushing

- Use a **soft bee brush** to gently sweep bees off each frame
- Do this over the hive to allow bees to fall back into the box
- Place cleaned frames into a covered container or box to keep them bee-free

Note: Effective, but **time-consuming** and may agitate the bees if not done calmly and carefully.

Straining, Bottling & Labeling Your Honey

You've harvested your honey—now it's time to clean it up and store it properly. Whether you're keeping it for yourself or sharing with friends (or customers), here's how to finish the process like a pro.

1. Straining Your Honey

After extracting (or slicing) the honey, strain it to remove:

- Wax particles
- Bee parts (it's rare but happens)
- Debris from the comb

How to Do It:

- Use a **fine mesh strainer** or **cheesecloth**
- Let honey flow into a **food-grade bucket**
- Cover and allow to **settle for 24–48 hours** so air bubbles rise and debris separates

This settling period gives you **cleaner, clearer honey**.

2. Bottling the Honey

Choose clean, food-safe containers like:

- Glass jars
- Mason jars
- Squeeze bottles

Before Bottling:

- Sanitize containers with warm water or a gentle food-safe rinse
- Use a **honey gate** or ladle for pouring
- Fill jars and **seal tightly**

Storage Tips:

- Keep honey at **room temperature**, away from direct sunlight
- Avoid the fridge—**cold causes crystallization**

3. Labeling Your Honey (Even for Gifts)

If you plan to **give, sell, or share** your honey:

- Include **harvest date** and **honey type** (e.g., Wildflower, Clover)
- State if it's **raw** or **unpasteurized** (if applicable)
- Add your **name, brand, or contact info**
- Mention any **possible allergen traces**, such as pollen or bee-derived materials

If selling, follow your **local food labeling laws**. Requirements vary by state or country.

Selling Honey Legally

Turning liquid gold into income—by the book

So, your bees have been working hard, and now you've got jars of rich, golden honey. Naturally, you might be thinking: "Can I sell this?" The answer is: **Yes, you can!** But before you start slapping on labels and selling at the local market, there are a few important legal steps to follow to make sure you're doing it **safely and legally**.

Step 1: Understand Cottage Food Laws in Your State

In the U.S., many small food producers (like backyard beekeepers) are protected by something called **"Cottage Food Laws."** These laws allow you to make and sell certain foods from your home kitchen—without needing a commercial license. **Honey** is often on that list, but each state has its own specific rules.

Here's what you'll typically need to check:

Key Questions:

- Is labeling required?

  Most states require you to include:

  - Product name (e.g., "Raw Wildflower Honey")
  - Your name & address (or business name)
  - Net weight (in ounces and grams)
  - Allergen statement (if applicable)
  - A note like "This product was made in a home kitchen not subject to inspection"

- Are health inspections needed?

  In many cases, honey is exempt from inspections, but if you plan to scale up or sell outside your home (like at retail stores), an inspection or certification may be required.

- Where can you sell your honey?

  This varies by state:

  - Farmers' markets
  - Roadside stands
  - Local fairs
  - Direct from your home
  - Online (some states restrict this under cottage laws)

Pro tip: Visit your state's Department of Agriculture or Department of Health website and search "cottage food laws" + "honey." Some states (like Texas, Florida, and California) have their own honey-specific regulations.

Step 2: Cover the Business Basics

Even if you're starting small, treating your honey venture like a micro-business sets you up for long-term success.

Here's what you'll want to do:

- **Register a business name** (also called a DBA or "Doing Business As") if you want to sell under a brand like *"Sweet Creek Honey Co."*
  - Check with your county or state on how to register.

- **Use food-grade, sealed containers**

  - Customers trust clean, professional packaging.
  - Don't reuse containers or use lids without seals for commercial sales.

- **Label your honey clearly**

- o Avoid making **unproven health claims** (like "cures allergies" or "heals wounds")—these can get you into legal trouble.
- **Flavored or infused honey?**
  - o Adding cinnamon, vanilla, lemon, CBD, or other ingredients **may classify your product as processed**, requiring different licenses or inspections.
  - o Always check local food processing rules before selling infused honey.

- **Keep detailed records**

  - o Note your **harvest dates, batch weights, number of jars produced, and where/when each batch was sold.**
  - o This helps with inventory, builds credibility, and keeps you covered in case of questions or recalls.

Pro tip: Join a Local Beekeeping Association

Your local beekeepers' group can be one of your **greatest resources** for navigating the legal side of honey sales. These groups often:

- Share state-specific legal insights
- Offer low-cost liability insurance
- Host local honey contests or markets
- Connect you with bulk packaging suppliers
- Help with marketing and pricing advice

Some associations even have group licenses or cooperative bottling equipment to help new sellers get started affordably.

Wrapping up…

Harvesting honey is a sweet milestone in your beekeeping journey—but it's also a moment of reflection. Your bees worked hard for that honey, and with thoughtful timing, gentle methods, and respect for the colony's needs, you'll be able to enjoy the fruits of their labor without setting them back.

Remember: **always leave enough honey for the hive** to survive and thrive. A responsible harvest today leads to stronger bees tomorrow—and plenty more sweetness down the line.

Chapter 8:

Bee Pollinator Garden

Creating a Flower-Filled Paradise for Your Bees

Now that your bees have a safe, healthy hive and you've mastered the basics of colony care, it's time to look at what surrounds the hive: **the landscape.** Whether you're on a half-acre lot or just working with planters on a patio, **what you plant matters.** Bees don't just live in hives—they live in ecosystems. And as a beekeeper, you're not just managing bees… you're managing their world.

This chapter will show you how to build a **pollinator-friendly garden** that supports your bees *and* beautifies your space. You'll learn what to plant, when to plant it, how to keep it chemical-free, and how even the smallest garden can make a huge impact.

Why What You Plant Matters for Bee Health

A thriving honeybee colony doesn't just rely on sugar water and a patch of clover. While those help in a pinch, **healthy, productive bees** need a steady and varied diet throughout the entire foraging season—from early spring to late fall. Think of your bees like elite athletes: they're constantly working, flying for miles, and feeding thousands of mouths back at home. Their energy needs are enormous.

If the local landscape lacks floral diversity or if flowers bloom in a short burst and then disappear, your bees may struggle to:

- Raise strong, healthy brood
- Store enough honey for winter
- Fight off diseases and pests
- Avoid stress and colony collapse

Unfortunately, modern environments don't make it easy. **Monoculture farming, widespread use of pesticides, shrinking wildflower habitats, and manicured lawns** all mean fewer flowers and fewer food options. And that's a big reason why **both wild and managed bees** are in decline.

But here's the good news:
You can change that—right in your own garden.

No matter how small your space, from sprawling backyards to balcony planters, you can create a buzzing haven that helps your bees thrive.

What Do Bees Actually Eat?

Honeybees rely on **two key resources from plants**:

- **Nectar** – This is their main source of **carbohydrates**. Bees use nectar for energy, and they convert it into honey to feed the colony and survive the winter.
- **Pollen** – This is their **protein** source. It's crucial for raising new bees (brood), developing strong immune systems, and keeping the queen healthy and productive.

A healthy colony needs **both** in good supply. And just like humans, bees do better with variety.

Why Seasonal Blooms Matter

In nature, different plants bloom at different times. But in a typical garden, most people unknowingly plant flowers that **all bloom at once**, leaving huge food gaps before and after.

Your job? **Stagger the buffet**. You want to provide blooms from early spring to the last warm days of fall—because bees don't stop working just because summer ends.

Let's break it down by season, with plant suggestions that are easy to grow, bee-approved, and beginner-friendly.

Best Plants for Pollinators by Season

Your bees can only be as healthy as the environment you place them in—and flowers are their fuel. Nectar gives them energy (like sugar), and pollen gives them protein (for building bee bodies). Different plants bloom at different times of year, so planning a garden that offers **continuous blooms** is one of the most powerful things you can do to keep your colony thriving.

Let's walk through what to plant **by season** to give your bees what they need, exactly when they need it.

Spring (March–May)

Why this season matters:

After surviving winter, bees emerge **hungry, cold, and weak**. They desperately need **early nectar and pollen** to rebuild their strength and feed new larvae. The earlier your garden blooms, the better their chances of a strong start.

Plant These Early Bloomers:

- **Crocus** – One of the very first flowers to bloom, often peeking through snow.
- **Dandelion** – Yes, they're weeds—but to bees, they're a buffet. Don't mow them early!
- **Willow Trees** – Produce loads of pollen early on, critical for brood development.
- **Fruit Trees** – Apple, cherry, plum, and pear trees burst with nectar and pollen in early spring.
- **Maples** – Often bloom before leaves appear; bees love their early nectar and pollen.
- **Borage** – Re-seeds itself easily and produces flowers early and often.
- **Bluebells** – Great for shade and early forage. Plus, they look magical.

Summer (June–August)

Why this season matters:

Summer is **peak beekeeping season**. Bees are busy gathering nectar to make honey, raising young bees, and building wax comb. They need a steady supply of **high-nectar flowers** that bloom throughout these hot months.

Plant These Summer Favorites:

- **Lavender** – A bee favorite; blooms for weeks and smells divine.
- **Echinacea (Coneflower)** – With bold purple petals, they're hardy, drought-tolerant, and productive.
- **Black-eyed Susan** – Native to many regions and attracts bees by the dozens.
- **Bee Balm (Monarda)** – Fragrant and absolutely buzzing with pollinators when in bloom.
- **Clover (Red & White)** – Low-growing, nitrogen-fixing, and high in nectar.
- **Mint** – Let it flower! Bees go crazy for the blossoms.
- **Sunflowers** – Big pollen producers and a magnet for bees (plus, they look amazing in photos).

Fall (September–October)

Why this season matters:

As the weather cools, bees work hard to **store enough honey for winter**. But many plants are done blooming. That's why late-season flowers are so important—bees need one last burst of energy and nutrition before the cold sets in.

Plant These Fall Bloomers:

- **Goldenrod** – One of the most important fall nectar sources; don't pull it!
- **Asters** – These star-shaped flowers bloom late and come in a rainbow of colors.
- **Sedum ('Autumn Joy')** – A tough perennial that blooms right when bees need it most.

- **Joe Pye Weed** – Tall, native, and completely covered in bees in fall.
- **Zinnias** – Long-blooming annuals that bees (and butterflies) adore.
- **Marigolds** – Vibrant and helpful for bees, while also repelling some garden pests.

Pro tip: Go Native Whenever You Can

While all pollinator-friendly plants help, **native plants** are the gold standard.

Why?

Because they've evolved alongside **your region's bees**, which means:

- They bloom at exactly the right time for local pollinators
- They require **less water, fertilizer, and fuss**
- They attract **a wider variety of native bee species**, not just honeybees
- They're naturally more disease- and pest-resistant in your soil and climate

Where to find native plants:

- Your local **garden center or nursery**
- **State native plant societies**
- Free tools like **Pollinator Partnership's ecoregional planting guides** (www.pollinator.org)

What to Avoid (For the Sake of the Bees)

Even a well-planned pollinator garden can go wrong if you include the wrong elements. Here's what to leave out:

Pesticides & Herbicides

- Avoid anything labeled **"systemic"** or **"neonicotinoid"**—these chemicals are **absorbed into the plant**, so even the nectar and pollen become toxic to bees.
- Even some **organic products** can be dangerous—always read the label before spraying.

Double-Petal Hybrids

- These fancy-looking flowers are often **sterile**. They may look lush, but they offer **no nectar or pollen**.

Overly Manicured Lawns

- A perfectly green, weed-free lawn is a **bee desert**. Let clover, wild violets, and yes—even some dandelions—have a place in your yard.

Avoiding Pesticides and Chemicals

One of the unexpected joys of keeping bees is how your garden transforms. Flowers seem fuller. Fruits set more easily. Vegetables grow stronger. Your backyard becomes a small, living ecosystem—and it's not just you doing the work. Your bees are out there, pollinating, supporting growth, and bringing life to every bloom.

But here's a critical truth many new beekeepers overlook:

Even the most well-meaning gardener can accidentally poison their own hive.

Yes, really. Many common gardening products—even those labeled "natural" or "bee-safe"—contain ingredients that can **confuse, weaken, or kill bees**. The problem is that **harm isn't always immediate or obvious**. Sometimes, it starts small—affecting their ability to fly straight, find the hive, or remember flower locations. Other times, it compromises the entire colony's immune system or poisons developing larvae inside the hive.

Let's break down the major chemical culprits, why they're dangerous, and **what you can do instead** to create a safe, healthy, and buzzing garden.

Chemicals to Avoid—And Why

1. Pesticides (Insect Killers)

Pesticides are designed to kill insects—and bees *are* insects. While many products are targeted at garden pests like aphids, beetles, or caterpillars, they often don't discriminate between the "bad bugs" and the beneficial pollinators.

Bees exposed to pesticides may:

- Lose their ability to navigate
- Stop foraging
- Die mid-flight or inside the hive
- Bring contaminated pollen or nectar back to the colony

Common Offenders:

- Beetle and caterpillar sprays
- Ant and wasp killers
- "All-in-one" sprays for flower beds and veggies

Safer Alternatives:

- **Neem oil**: A plant-based oil that repels pests without harming bees (when used correctly)

- **Insecticidal soap**: Great for soft-bodied pests
- **Companion planting**: Use basil, marigolds, or mint to naturally repel harmful bugs
- **Manual removal**: Sometimes, a quick squish is safer than a spray

Timing tip: Always apply treatments at **dusk**, when bees have returned to the hive.

2. Herbicides (Weed Killers)

These products, like glyphosate-based brands (e.g., Roundup), are used to eliminate unwanted weeds—but some of those "weeds" (like clover or dandelions) are **critical early-season food** for your bees.

Herbicides can also:

- Harm **soil microbes** that plants and fungi depend on
- Linger in the soil and affect surrounding vegetation
- Indirectly reduce bee foraging options by eliminating nectar sources

What to Do Instead:

- Embrace "weeds" like clover, chickweed, and dandelions in early spring
- Use a **hoe or mulch** to manage garden beds
- Let patches of wildflowers or native grass grow in corners of your yard

3. Fungicides (Mold & Mildew Control)

Often forgotten, fungicides are used to prevent or treat fungal issues in the garden—but many are **not tested for bee safety**, and some have been shown to:

- **Disrupt the bee gut microbiome**, leading to weakened immunity
- Affect **larval development** in the hive
- Increase toxicity when combined with other chemicals (like pesticides)

Fungicides are especially dangerous when sprayed on **flowering plants**, as residues may collect in nectar and pollen.

Better Options:

- Prune for airflow
- Water at the base of plants (not on the leaves)
- Use **baking soda + water spray** as a mild fungicide

The Hidden Danger: Systemic Pesticides

Unlike sprays that coat the surface of leaves or flowers, **systemic pesticides** are absorbed into the plant itself. They're used on seeds, roots, or leaves and **travel through the entire system**—meaning the toxin ends up in:

- Pollen
- Nectar
- Water droplets on leaves

Bees can't see or smell these residues. They unknowingly gather them and bring them into the hive, where they can:

- Poison larvae
- Harm the queen
- Weaken the whole colony over time

Watch Out for Neonicotinoids

This class of systemic insecticides is **particularly dangerous to bees**, even at low doses. They're found in many over-the-counter garden products—sometimes under different names.

Look for (and avoid) these active ingredients on labels:

- Imidacloprid
- Clothianidin
- Thiamethoxam
- Dinotefuran

Always read ingredient lists carefully, even on products labeled "natural" or "organic." Just because it's plant-based doesn't mean it's safe for bees.

Pro Tips to Keep Your Garden Bee-Safe

- If you must treat plants, do it **after sunset**, when bees are safely back in the hive.
- Never spray **blooming flowers**—this is where bees gather nectar and pollen.
- Keep a **clean water source** (like a shallow bowl with pebbles) to discourage bees from sipping chemical-contaminated puddles.
- Encourage **native plants** that are naturally resistant to pests and attract beneficial insects.

Companion Planting for Your Bees & Garden

When you hear the term *"companion planting,"* think of it like matchmaking in the garden. It's a centuries-old gardening practice where certain plants are placed close together because they help each other thrive—whether that's by repelling pests, improving soil health, or enhancing growth.

But here's where it gets even more exciting for beekeepers: **many of the best companion plants are also pollinator powerhouses.** That means you can grow stronger veggies, reduce harmful pests naturally, and give your bees a banquet—all in one move.

Why Companion Planting Matters for Bees

Bees need nectar and pollen sources that are diverse, abundant, and available through the growing season—not just when your vegetables are flowering. Companion plants can:

- **Provide continuous forage** when crops aren't blooming
- **Attract bees to your veggie plants**, boosting pollination
- **Keep harmful pests in check**, reducing the need for chemicals that harm your hive
- **Support biodiversity**, creating a healthier ecosystem around your apiary

It's nature's version of multi-tasking.

Top Bee-Loving Companion Plants (and Why They Rock)

Here's a short list of some **bee-friendly plants** that make excellent companions in your vegetable garden—plus what else they do to help.

Plant	Bee Benefit	Garden Bonus
Borage	One of bees' all-time favorites. Blooms repeatedly through the season.	Repels tomato hornworms. Self-seeds easily for next year.
Basil	When allowed to flower, it attracts bees in droves.	Deters aphids, flies, and even mosquitoes. Great for tomatoes.
Calendula	Loaded with pollen and blooms long into fall.	Attracts pollinators, improves soil, and helps trap bad bugs.
Marigold	Vibrant blooms draw bees and hoverflies.	Excellent pest repellent: deters nematodes, whiteflies, and beetles.
Nasturtium	Bees love its bright flowers; blooms early.	Acts as a "trap crop" for aphids and whiteflies—keeping them off your veggies. Leaves and flowers are edible!

Garden Tip:

Interplant these flowers among or around your crops like tomatoes, cucumbers, beans, and peppers. This draws bees in to pollinate the entire area while reducing the need for chemical sprays.

How to Place Them in Your Garden (No Experience Needed)

Here's how even a complete beginner can start companion planting for bees:

1. **Border Your Garden with Blooms** – Line the edges with marigold, calendula, or nasturtium to attract pollinators and repel bugs from the outside in.
2. **Tuck Flowers Between Rows** – Plant basil, borage, or nasturtium between rows of vegetables like cucumbers or peppers to keep pest levels low and bee activity high.
3. **Group in Trios or Clusters** – Bees prefer groupings of flowers over scattered singles. Plant 3–5 of each type in small clusters for better visibility.
4. **Let Some Herbs Flower** – Don't harvest all your basil or oregano. Let a few go to flower to feed your pollinators.
5. **Rotate and Reseed** – Many of these plants self-seed (especially borage and calendula). Let them spread naturally and replant as needed each season.

A small vegetable garden showing tomatoes, cucumbers, and peppers surrounded by companion flowers like borage, marigold, and nasturtium with bees flying between them

Creating a Nectar & Pollen-Rich Landscape

One of the kindest—and smartest—things you can do for your bees is to create a **diverse and flower-rich environment**. While bees will forage up to three miles away, they always prefer **easy, nearby access** to a reliable food source. By planting a continuous supply of nectar- and pollen-rich plants in your yard, garden, or even containers, you're not just helping your hive—you're also supporting wild pollinators and increasing biodiversity.

Here's how to build a **bee-friendly landscape** step by step.

Start With Structure: Trees & Shrubs

Think of trees and shrubs as the **backbone of your bee garden**. They bloom early—just when bees are waking up—and offer **huge amounts of nectar and pollen** in each bloom cycle. Unlike small flowers, a single tree can feed thousands of bees at once.

Here are some excellent options:

- **Linden (Basswood):** Often called the "bee tree," its summer flowers are rich in nectar and have a sweet fragrance that bees can't resist.
- **Hawthorn:** Blooms early in spring when forage is scarce, giving your colony a much-needed kickstart.
- **Sumac:** A hardy shrub with cone-shaped flowers full of pollen—great for building bee strength.
- **Raspberries & Blackberries:** Not only are they loved by bees, but they give *you* delicious fruit, too. Win-win!

Layer in Perennials: Long-Term, Low Maintenance

Perennials come back year after year and require less water and care once established. They're the **reliable workers** of your pollinator garden, blooming across different times of the growing season.

Try these favorites:

- **Yarrow:** Flat-topped flowers make landing easy; blooms throughout summer.
- **Bee Balm (Monarda):** True to its name—bees, butterflies, and hummingbirds all adore it.
- **Lupine:** Adds nitrogen to your soil and vertical visual appeal to your beds.
- **Blanketflower (Gaillardia):** Long bloom time and a vibrant burst of color that attracts foragers.

Don't Forget Herbs (Let Them Flower!)

Many new gardeners grow herbs for cooking—but if you let them bloom, **they become powerful bee magnets**. Plus, herbs are often drought-tolerant and easy to grow in containers or small spaces.

Bees love:

- **Thyme:** A groundcover with tiny pink-purple blossoms full of nectar.

- **Oregano:** Let it flower and it'll buzz with activity for weeks.
- **Lemon Balm:** Part of the mint family—spreads easily and smells amazing.
- **Chives:** Edible for you, delightful for bees when left to bloom.

Brighten Things Up with Annuals

Annuals are **fast-growing, season-long bloomers** that provide instant color and foraging value. They're perfect for filling in gaps between perennial blooms or container planting.

Add these to your mix:

- **Cosmos:** Airy and easy to grow—especially attractive to bees and butterflies.
- **Zinnias:** Bright, bold, and long-lasting. Great for cutting gardens, too.
- **Sunflowers:** A favorite of bees *and* birds. Choose multi-headed varieties for extended bloom time.
- **Sweet Alyssum:** Small but mighty—produces tons of nectar in cool seasons.

Garden Design Tip: Think Big, Not Scattered

Bees are efficient foragers. They're drawn to **large, obvious patches** of blooms rather than single, isolated plants.

Plant flowers in blocks or clumps, ideally **at least 3 ft x 3 ft per variety**. This lets bees forage more efficiently and encourages them to stick around longer.

Final Touches: Water, Soil, and Wild Spaces

Feeding your bees isn't just about flowers. A truly bee-friendly yard also offers access to clean water, nesting spaces for wild bees, and a little touch of natural "messiness."

Water Source: Every Hive Needs One

Bees need water to cool the hive, dilute honey, and digest food. But they're picky—they won't land on open water without somewhere to perch.

Try this:

- Use a **shallow dish, birdbath, or saucer** filled with pebbles, corks, or twigs
- Change the water **every few days** to avoid mosquito larvae
- Place it in a **sunny, accessible spot** near the hive

Leave Some Soil Bare for Native Bees

Not all bees live in hives. In fact, **70% of native bee species** nest in the ground. If your yard is fully mulched or covered in landscape fabric, they'll have nowhere to burrow.

What to do:

- Leave a few small patches of **bare, undisturbed soil**
- Choose a sunny, sloped area that drains well
- **Avoid pesticides** and compaction (no foot traffic or heavy equipment)

This simple act invites dozens of solitary bee species into your space—many of which are **even more effective pollinators than honeybees.**

Let It Grow a Little Wild

It might feel counterintuitive, but a bit of "wild" is good for bees.

Try this:

- Leave **dead stems** standing over winter—many bees nest inside them
- Allow a corner of your yard to go a bit **untamed**
- Let some **dandelions, clover, or violets** grow freely—they're early and late-season food sources
- Skip over-cleaning leaf litter—it's habitat for beneficial insects

Creating a sanctuary for bees doesn't mean giving up beauty. In fact, many bee-friendly gardens are among the **most vibrant, buzzing, and alive** spaces you'll ever visit.

Making a Mini Bee Paradise

Think you need a big backyard to keep your bees happy? Think again! Even if you're working with a **tiny balcony, rooftop nook, or small patio**, you can still create a buzzing little oasis that gives your bees the nectar, pollen, and hydration they need to thrive.

The key is being **intentional** with the space you have. A few well-placed plants, herbs, and water sources can turn even a compact area into a rich buffet for your bees.

Here's how to do it:

Bee-Friendly Flower Ideas for Tight Spaces:

Even a **window box** or **potted plant** can make a difference. Choose **pollen- and nectar-rich blooms** that are easy to grow and bloom across multiple seasons. Mixing 2–3 flower types in a container ensures variety for your bees and color for your space!

Try these:

- **Lavender**: Beautiful, drought-resistant, and loved by bees
- **Calendula**: Easy to grow and blooms for months
- **Black-eyed Susan**: Hardy and attractive to pollinators
- **Zinnias**: Colorful, long-blooming, and beginner-friendly

Place these in window boxes or small pots along sunny sills or railings.

Grow Herbs Bees Love

Small-space gardening isn't just about flowers—**culinary herbs** are bee favorites too. They're easy to grow in **railing planters**, **hanging baskets**, or even **old mugs** on your windowsill!

Bee-attracting herbs include:

- **Thyme**
- **Basil**
- **Mint**
- **Oregano**
- **Chives**

Let some of your herbs go to flower—this is when they're most attractive to bees!

Use Hanging Baskets & Trellises

No ground space? Go vertical! Hanging baskets and wall-mounted planters make great pollinator stations.

Here's what to try:

- **Nasturtiums**: Edible, vibrant, and irresistible to bees
- **Sweet alyssum**: Small, fragrant flowers bees adore
- **Morning glory** or **scarlet runner beans**: Fast-growing vines that love a trellis and bloom like crazy

Install a lightweight trellis on a sunny wall or balcony rail to maximize space.

Add a Bee Bath

Bees need water—but not deep bowls! They need **shallow water sources** where they can **land safely and sip** without drowning.

Try this simple DIY:

- Use a shallow dish or plant saucer
- Add small pebbles, glass beads, or cork pieces for perches

- Fill with fresh water, just to the top of the pebbles
- Refresh daily, especially in summer

Place your bee bath in a sunny, visible area near your plants.

No Chemicals—Ever

Avoid **pesticides, herbicides, and chemical sprays** at all costs—even those labeled "natural." These are toxic to bees and other beneficial insects.

If pests are an issue, use organic techniques like:

- Hand removal
- Neem oil (only at night, when bees aren't active)
- Companion planting to deter unwanted bugs

Stagger Your Blooms

Plan your planting so something is always blooming—from early spring through late fall. Bees need a **continuous food supply**, not just a one-time floral show.

You can do this by:

- Choosing varieties with different bloom times
- Replacing spent plants mid-season
- Adding perennials that return each year at different times

Think of your space as a pollinator calendar—spring, summer, and fall should all be represented!

Final Buzz: Every Little Bit Helps

Even one flowering pot on a windowsill can support dozens of pollinators in your neighborhood. By planting with purpose, you're not just helping your own hive—you're becoming part of a **bigger movement to protect pollinators** everywhere.

Whether you have a full backyard or just a balcony, you can be a bee hero.

Wrapping up…

Creating a pollinator-friendly garden is one of the most beautiful and rewarding parts of being a beekeeper. It's where you become more than a honey harvester—you become a **pollinator protector**.

By planting with purpose, avoiding toxins, and offering seasonal blooms, you're not just feeding your bees—you're **healing ecosystems**, **supporting biodiversity**, and **beautifying your corner of the planet**.

Chapter 9:

Troubleshooting & Growing with Confidence

From rookie mistakes to raising queens — here's how to keep going, growing, and thriving

By this point, you've done a lot: you've learned how bees work, set up your apiary, chosen the right hive, cared for your colony, and maybe even harvested your first golden jar of honey. But let's be honest—beekeeping isn't always sunshine and nectar. Sometimes things go sideways.

This chapter is your safety net. Here, we'll explore **common mistakes**, teach you how to recover when something goes wrong, and show you how to evolve from a beginner to a confident, skilled beekeeper ready to take the next step—whether that means more hives or raising queens.

Top Mistakes New Beekeepers Make

Here's a secret every experienced beekeeper will tell you: **mistakes are part of the journey**. They're not signs of failure—they're signs of learning. Even the most seasoned beekeepers have made choices they regret (hello, forgotten mite checks). What matters most is **spotting problems early**, knowing **what to look for**, and being willing to course-correct with confidence.

This chapter walks you through the **most common beginner beekeeping mistakes**, how to **recognize warning signs**, and what steps to take to recover fast. We'll also talk about when to call for backup—and how to keep growing as your skills (and your bees) evolve.

Mistake #1: Skipping Regular Hive Inspections

It's totally normal to be nervous at first. Some beginners worry about "bothering the bees" or getting stung, so they avoid opening the hive. Unfortunately, skipping inspections means missing the early signs of problems.

Why It Matters:

Regular hive checks (every **10–14 days** during spring and summer) allow you to monitor:

- **Queen health** (Is she laying eggs?)
- **Brood pattern** (Is it consistent and healthy?)
- **Pest/disease activity** (Are mites, beetles, or wax moths present?)
- **Swarm preparations** (Queen cells being built?)

- **Food stores** (Enough honey and pollen?)

What to Do:

Learn to inspect with **calm, deliberate movements**. Wear protective gear, work in mild weather, and keep smoke gentle. Bees adjust to your presence over time—and so will your nerves.

Mistake #2: Overfeeding or Underfeeding

Feeding is crucial—especially in **early spring**, **drought**, or **fall prep**. But too much or too little can cause problems.

Underfeeding Risks:

- Starvation during nectar dearths
- Brood disruption due to lack of resources

Overfeeding Risks:

- Hive congestion (not enough space for the queen to lay)
- Moisture buildup from excess syrup
- Stimulated brood production at the wrong time (like late fall)

What to Do:

Feed **only when needed**. Use your inspections to check for:

- Frame weight (are they heavy with honey?)
- Brood patterns (are they expanding too much?)
- Pollen stores (do bees have enough protein sources?)

Mistake #3: Missing Signs of a Failing Queen

A weak or missing queen can spiral into colony collapse if left unchecked. But new beekeepers often miss the early signs.

What to Watch For:

- No eggs or larvae
- Patchy or spotty brood pattern
- Increased aggression in worker bees
- More drones than usual (drone-laying workers)
- Queen cells being built unexpectedly

What to Do:

- Know what a **healthy brood frame** looks like: full, tight, and consistent.
- Compare side-by-side photos in your beekeeping manual or online groups.
- If in doubt, **ask a mentor** or local inspector to take a look.

Mistake #4: Ignoring Varroa Mite Management

Varroa destructor may sound like a comic book villain—but it's very real, and very deadly. These microscopic parasites feed on bee fat bodies and transmit viruses. Most new beekeepers **underestimate their impact** until it's too late.

What to Do:

- Test for mites **monthly** using the **sugar roll** or **alcohol wash** method.
- Learn your treatment options: organic (oxalic acid, formic acid) or synthetic.
- Follow thresholds: when mite loads exceed **3 mites per 100 bees**, it's time to act.

Pro tip: Even treatment-free beekeepers **test regularly** and cull colonies with uncontrolled infestations.

Mistake #5: Harvesting Honey Too Early

That golden nectar is tempting—but harvesting too early can **doom your bees to starvation**, especially heading into winter.

What to Do:

- Only harvest when bees have **capped** honey cells.
- Leave at least **60–80 lbs** of honey in the hive for winter (this varies by climate).
- Use a **hive scale** or count the number of full, capped frames.

Bees come first—always. A strong, well-fed colony = more honey next year.

When to Call a Mentor or Join a Beekeeping Group

You've read the guides, watched the tutorials, and maybe even assembled your hive. But when it comes to **real-life beekeeping**, nothing beats having someone you can turn to with your hands in the hive and a dozen buzzing questions in your head.

That's where beekeeping mentors and communities come in.

Whether you're dealing with a confusing hive inspection, wondering if your queen is missing, or just unsure if that weird white fuzz is mold or wax, a quick message or chat with someone experienced can save you time, stress, and even your colony.

Why Join a Beekeeping Community?

Beekeeping is not meant to be a solo journey—especially in the beginning. Local clubs and online groups are full of friendly folks who have *been where you are* and are eager to help you succeed.

Here's what you gain when you connect with a beekeeping group:

Real-Time, Seasoned Advice

Get practical, honest answers from people who've managed hives in your climate, your region, and your exact situation. They've seen swarms, mites, missing queens, honey overflow—and everything in between.

Hands-On Learning & Workshops

Many local clubs host hive tours, in-person meetups, and beginner workshops where you can suit up and **learn by doing**—not just reading. You'll gain confidence quickly with a smoker in your hand and a mentor at your side.

Mentorship & On-Site Support

Some associations will pair you with an experienced keeper who can visit your hive, walk you through inspections, and help you troubleshoot tricky problems in real time.

Local Disease & Pest Alerts

Diseases and pests often move regionally. Your local group will alert you when there's a **Varroa mite outbreak**, **foulbrood warning**, or **swarming season peak**—things you may not learn from a book until it's too late.

A Bee-Loving Community

Beekeepers are a unique bunch. Whether you're nerding out over comb patterns or panicking about a queenless hive, it's comforting to have people who understand your passion—and your challenges.

Pro tip: Start with your state's **beekeeping association** or **agricultural extension office**—they often list local clubs and regional chapters. Many groups welcome beginners and even offer **free mentor programs** for new members.

Top U.S. Beekeeping Associations & Mentor Resources for Beginners

1. American Beekeeping Federation (ABF)

Website: https://www.abfnet.org
One of the largest national beekeeping organizations. Offers educational materials, youth scholarships, webinars, and annual conferences.
Use their **"Find a Beekeeper"** tool and **state affiliate directory** to locate clubs and mentors.

2. Bee Culture Magazine – Beekeeping Events & Club Listings

Website: https://www.beeculture.com
Offers a large, frequently updated list of beekeeping clubs by state. Great for finding **local meetings, classes, and field days** near you.
Visit their **"Bee Club Listings"** page under Resources.

3. Your State's Agricultural Extension Office

How to Find: Google "[Your State] + Cooperative Extension + Beekeeping"
Example: Texas Cooperative Extension Beekeeping
State university extensions often run **free or low-cost beekeeping programs**, and many provide **hands-on field days and master beekeeper courses**. They also usually track **local disease alerts** and legislation updates.

4. Local & Regional Beekeeping Associations

Here are a few strong state-level examples (you can look up your own if it's not listed):

- **California State Beekeepers Association** – https://www.californiastatebeekeepers.com
- **Texas Beekeepers Association** – https://texasbeekeepers.org
- **Florida State Beekeepers Association** – https://www.floridabeekeepers.org
- **New York State Beekeepers** – https://www.escba.org

Most have **mentor matching programs**, seasonal workshops, and newsletters.

5. BeeSource Community Forums

Website: https://www.beesource.com/forums
One of the largest online beekeeping forums in the world. Great for **asking questions**, sharing photos, and getting quick feedback from seasoned beekeepers.

6. Facebook Beekeeping Groups (with Regional Focus)

Search for groups like:

- Backyard Beekeepers of [Your State]
- First-Year Beekeepers
- Natural Beekeeping Conversations

- Beekeeping Questions and Answers

Look for **active moderation** and large membership for the best experience.

7. The Bee Informed Partnership (BIP)

Website: https://beeinformed.org
A research-driven organization that helps beekeepers with **data-backed hive health tracking**, seasonal management tips, and pest alerts by region.

8. Meetup.com – Search "Beekeeping"

Many hobbyist and local clubs host **events, hive tours, or classes** via Meetup. It's a great option if you're in a city or suburban area and want informal group learning.

Bottom line?

Don't wait until you're overwhelmed, frustrated, or confused to reach out. The beekeeping world is full of kind, experienced people who remember exactly what it felt like to be new—and they're ready to guide you.

Even one good conversation can make the difference between giving up and growing stronger as a beekeeper.

What to Do When Things Go Wrong

Let's be real: no matter how careful or prepared you are, **something will go wrong** at some point. But here's the truth: most beekeeping "crises" aren't disasters—they're puzzles. And lucky for you, they all come with clues.

The #1 rule in beekeeping when something feels off?

Don't panic. Pause, observe, then act.

Bees are **incredibly resilient creatures**. They've been around for over 100 million years and have seen it all—droughts, predators, bad weather, even volcanoes. Your job isn't to be perfect. It's to pay attention, trust your observations, and take thoughtful, timely action.

Here's a breakdown of **common problem scenarios** you may run into, what they typically mean, and what to do about them.

No Eggs or Larvae in the Hive

What It Might Mean:

- Your queen may be **dead**, **failing**, or **absent**
- It could also mean she's **not laying yet** if newly introduced

What To Do:

- First, check for the queen (visually or for signs of recent laying)
- If she's missing or clearly failing, you have two options:
    1. **Requeen** with a mated queen from a reputable source
    2. **Merge** with another hive that has a strong queen using the newspaper method (explained in later chapters)

Tips for Handling Hive Issues:

- **Keep a hive journal.** Record weather, behavior, and changes—it helps you spot patterns.
- **Inspect regularly, but don't overdo it.** Every 10–14 days during active seasons is usually enough.
- **Ask for help.** Join a local beekeeping group or online forum—beekeepers love to share wisdom.
- **Don't rush.** Sometimes doing nothing is better than doing the wrong thing in a hurry.

Bees Are Suddenly Aggressive

What It Might Mean:

- Your queen could have been replaced by a more defensive strain
- The hive might be getting **robbed** by other bees
- Weather, predators, or recent disturbances may have triggered stress

What To Do:

- Inspect the hive calmly and thoroughly
- If robbing is suspected:
    o Reduce the entrance size
    o Avoid feeding openly near the hive
- If aggression persists:
    o Consider **requeening** to introduce gentler genetics
    o Ensure you're using **calm handling** and avoiding unnecessary disruptions

White Crystals on Frames

What It Might Mean:

- This is usually just **sugar syrup crystallizing**
- It happens when feed isn't fully consumed or humidity is high

What To Do:

- Reduce or pause feeding, especially in cold or damp weather
- Check that your hive has **good ventilation**
- Clean affected frames if buildup is excessive

Bees Are Disappearing

What It Might Mean:

- The colony may have **swarmed**
- There may be **Colony Collapse Disorder (CCD)** or pesticide exposure
- Could also be natural die-off if it's late fall/winter

What To Do:

- Inspect the brood nest: is there capped brood? Eggs? Queen?
- Check the ground and surrounding plants for signs of pesticide poisoning
- Ask local farmers or gardeners if spraying occurred nearby
- In case of swarm: check trees, bushes, or structures near your hive

Spotty or Drone-Only Brood Pattern

What It Might Mean:

- Likely causes:
  - A **failing queen** laying unfertilized (drone) eggs
  - A **laying worker** in a queenless hive

What To Do:

- Look for the queen. If you can't find her and there's only drone brood, you're likely queenless.
- Check for **multiple eggs per cell** (a sign of laying workers)
- The solution:
  - **Shake out the bees** away from the hive and introduce a new queen or brood frame with eggs from another hive to encourage them to raise a new queen.
  - In some cases, it's easier to **combine** with another queenright hive.

Expanding to More Hives

After your first full season of beekeeping, something starts to happen. You've gained confidence. You've learned to read your bees. You've even harvested your first jar of golden honey. And then… you catch yourself daydreaming about another hive. Sound familiar?

You're not alone. Many first-time beekeepers quickly realize that **one hive is great—but two can be even better.**

Let's explore why expanding your apiary is a smart move—and what you need to consider before taking that leap.

Why Start a Second Hive?

Adding another hive isn't just about more bees or more honey. It actually **makes you a better, more resilient beekeeper.** Here's why:

1. Compare Hive Performance

Every colony behaves a little differently—even under the same conditions. With two hives, you'll be able to:

- **Observe side-by-side differences** in queen strength, temperament, and foraging habits
- **Learn faster** by watching how each colony responds to weather, pests, and seasonal changes

2. Provide Backup in an Emergency

One of the most valuable reasons to keep more than one hive? **Colony support.**

- You can move frames of **brood**, **honey**, or even **bees** from a strong hive to help a weak one.
- If a queen dies or fails, you may be able to **give the queenless hive an egg or young larva** to raise a new queen.

This kind of hive-to-hive sharing is impossible with just one colony.

3. Reduce the Risk of Total Loss

If your only hive collapses due to mites, disease, or queen issues, that's the end of your beekeeping season. But with two hives:

- You **spread the risk**
- You can **salvage resources** (equipment, bees, even drawn comb)
- You're not starting from scratch if one fails

4. Increase Honey Harvests

Let's not forget the sweet stuff. More hives = more bees = **more honey**. A healthy second hive can double or even triple your yield depending on conditions and management.

Expansion Comes with Responsibility

Of course, more bees = more work. Before you go all-in, understand what a second hive will require from you:

More Equipment

You'll need:

- Another hive setup (boxes, frames, base, lid)
- A second set of tools and a smoker (or at least a larger one)
- Possibly more protective gear if sharing among family or helpers

More Time

Two hives doesn't mean twice the work—but it's definitely **more frequent inspection time**, especially during swarm season, splits, or honey harvesting.

More Pest & Mite Management

Monitoring varroa mites, small hive beetles, or wax moths takes extra vigilance. Each hive may respond differently to treatments or infestations.

Higher Upfront Costs

Depending on your setup, the second hive can cost **$200–$500+**. But remember: it's also an investment in knowledge, resilience, and (eventually) honey.

Pro Tips: How to Expand the Smart Way

- **Plan Ahead**

  Don't wait until your first hive swarms or crashes to scramble for gear. It's much easier (and cheaper) to have your second hive equipment ready in advance.

- **Leave Space for Expansion**

  When choosing your hive locations, leave at least **3–6 feet** between hives for air circulation and ease of access during inspections.

- **Stagger Hive Orientations**

  Slightly turn the entrances away from each other. This prevents drifting (where bees accidentally enter the wrong hive), which can spread disease or robbing behavior.

- **Learn First, Then Expand**

   It's best to complete **one full season** with a single hive before jumping to two. That way, you've learned the basics, seen the seasonal flow, and understand what's involved.

Raising Your Own Queens

Once you've gained confidence managing a single hive—or if you're planning to expand your apiary—**raising your own queens** is a natural and exciting next step.

It's not only a practical way to reduce reliance on buying bees from outside suppliers, but it's also **one of the most fascinating processes in beekeeping**. Watching a tiny egg become a royal matriarch that will lead an entire colony? That's magic—and you can do it.

Why Raise Your Own Queen Bees?

- **Cost-effective**: Buying queens can be expensive, especially for multiple hives.
- **Control traits**: You can select bees that are more **docile, disease-resistant**, or **productive**—whatever suits your local conditions or goals.
- **Emergency readiness**: If your queen dies unexpectedly or fails, you'll know how to respond.
- **Deepens your skill**: Raising queens helps you understand colony dynamics on a whole new level.

What You'll Need (Beginner-Level)

While full-scale queen rearing—like grafting larvae or using cell builders—is an advanced skill, **you can start small**. Many beginners successfully raise queens using simple techniques like **splits** or by encouraging the hive to raise its own queen.

Here's what it takes:

1. A Strong Donor Colony

Choose a healthy, established hive that consistently shows:

- Calm behavior during inspections (gentleness)
- Steady honey and brood production
- No signs of disease or pests

This colony will provide the eggs or young larvae that can develop into new queens.

2. Nurse Bees

These are young worker bees (typically 5–10 days old) who specialize in feeding larvae. You'll need a group of nurse bees to **feed and care for the developing queen larvae** in their queen cells.

If you're doing a split, make sure the new hive has a good ratio of nurse bees—it's like sending the queen-to-be to her own royal daycare.

3. A Mating Nuc or Hive Split

You can place queen cells into a **mating nucleus hive (nuc)**—a small hive that holds just a few frames—or into a **hive split**. These setups serve as a temporary home for the new queen to emerge, mature, go on mating flights, and eventually begin laying.

Splitting an existing hive into two is one of the easiest methods to raise a queen naturally.

4. Drone Availability Nearby

Here's the part many beginners forget: **a virgin queen needs to mate with 10–20 drones** in mid-air mating flights to become fully fertile.

That means there need to be **enough mature drones** (male bees) in your area, typically from other colonies. Drones are seasonal, so queen-raising works best **in late spring or early summer**, when drones are plentiful.

Easy Entry: Let the Hive Do It

Did you know that hives can raise a new queen **on their own**, without any help from you?

This is called a **supersedure**—when the colony senses the current queen is failing or aging and they raise a replacement.

Here's what to do:

- If you notice large peanut-shaped queen cells along the face of brood frames, **don't panic**. This is likely supersedure, not swarming.
- Observe the process. Take notes. Let the colony handle it.
- Watch for the new queen to emerge, mate, and begin laying (this can take 2–3 weeks).

Pro tip: This is one of the best ways to learn queen biology naturally, without any intervention.

Building Long-Term Beekeeping Skills

Beekeeping isn't something you master in one season. It's a living, evolving craft that deepens over time—just like a garden or a sourdough starter. You'll find that **every year brings new lessons**, every hive behaves a little differently, and **nature always has the final say**. That's the beauty of it.

In the beginning, you might feel like you're constantly reacting—figuring things out as you go. But over time, you'll start to **anticipate the rhythm of the hive**, spot problems early, and trust your instincts. Here's how to **grow from a beginner to a confident, seasoned beekeeper**:

Keep a Beekeeping Journal

Write down everything: hive inspections, dates you added supers, how the bees behaved, what the weather was like, how much honey you harvested, and what treatments (if any) you applied.

Over time, this becomes your most valuable resource—**a personalized history of your own beekeeping journey** that helps you notice patterns, avoid past mistakes, and make better decisions year after year.

Read Seasonal Beekeeping Guides

Beekeeping changes with the seasons. What you do in spring (like preventing swarms and building up colony strength) is very different from your fall responsibilities (like preparing for winter and monitoring mite loads).
Learn the flow of the year so you're always one step ahead instead of playing catch-up.

Attend Beekeeping Classes or Conferences

You don't need a degree to become a great beekeeper—but learning from others will fast-track your growth.
Many areas offer:

- Local bee club meetings
- Online webinars
- State fairs with apiary booths
- Affordable "bee schools" or short workshops

These give you a chance to hear **real-world experience**, ask questions, and connect with others who love bees as much as you do.

Try New Techniques and Methods

Once you're comfortable with the basics, don't be afraid to explore:

- **Top-bar or Warre hives** for a more natural approach
- **Treatment-free beekeeping**, if you want a hands-off philosophy
- **Queen-rearing**, hive splits, or small-scale pollination services

These experiments make you **a more flexible, adaptable beekeeper**, ready to pivot when challenges come your way.

Teach Others What You Learn

It may sound surprising, but **the best way to learn is to teach**. Explaining beekeeping to someone else—whether a friend, neighbor, or child—forces you to simplify your thinking and understand your own knowledge gaps.
Start small: share what you've learned online, give a garden club talk, or help a new beekeeper install their first hive.

Be Kind to Yourself

Here's something you need to hear: **every beekeeper makes mistakes.** Everyone once struggled to light a smoker, dropped a frame, or panicked when they couldn't find the queen.

Confidence doesn't come from reading—it comes from **showing up, season after season**. With each hive, each year, and each mistake, you'll build intuition, patience, and a deeper connection to your bees.

You're not just growing honey. You're growing **wisdom**.

Wrapping up…

You've now stepped into the next phase of beekeeping—where experience shapes wisdom, and where you stop fearing problems and start solving them with clarity.

Mistakes? You'll still make a few. But now you know how to spot them, who to ask, and what to try next. More importantly, you've earned the insight to **grow beyond just keeping bees**—you're learning to **keep them well**.

Chapter 10:

Beyond Honey

By now, you've walked the full path—from setting up your hive and installing your bees to harvesting your first jars of liquid gold. But here's something even many experienced beekeepers overlook:

Your hive has **so much more to offer** than just honey.

This chapter explores the **other natural treasures** inside your hive—**beeswax, propolis, pollen**, and more—and shows you exactly how to collect, use, and store them. These bee byproducts aren't just nice-to-have; they're **versatile, valuable, and incredibly fun** to work with, whether you're crafting, selling, or simply using them at home.

What Else Your Hive Offers

While honey is the star of the show, the average healthy hive can also provide:

- **Beeswax**: Nature's waterproof, moldable wax with dozens of uses
- **Propolis**: A sticky, resinous substance bees use to disinfect their hive
- **Bee Pollen**: Protein-rich superfood harvested from flower visits
- **Royal Jelly** (rare, and more advanced): A milky substance fed to larvae and queens
- **Brood** (for advanced/ethnic culinary uses): Bee larvae eaten in some cultures, though not common in beginner-level beekeeping

Each of these products has **distinct benefits**, both in personal use and potential for small-scale income.

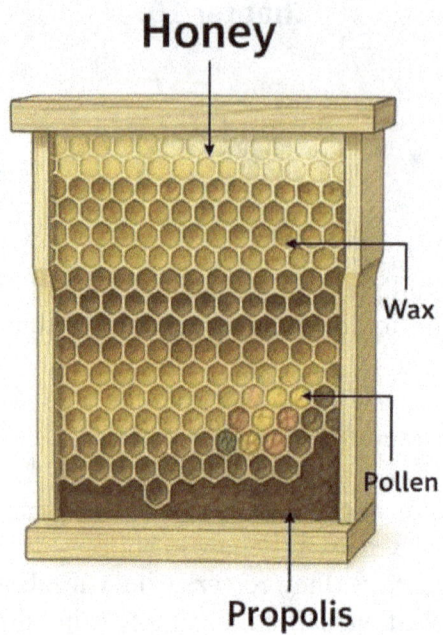

Honey

Wax

Pollen

Propolis

Image showing different hive products (honey, wax, pollen, propolis) and what part of the hive they come from.

Rendering Beeswax at Home

If honey is the sweet reward of beekeeping, **beeswax is the golden bonus.** Every time you harvest honey—especially when you **unseal the wax caps from your frames**—you're left with soft, fragrant, sticky wax that holds surprising value.

From candles to balms, beeswax has dozens of natural uses. But before you can turn it into anything useful, it needs to be **rendered**—or cleaned.

Rendering beeswax is a simple but satisfying process. It involves melting the raw wax to separate it from impurities like honey residue, dirt, bee parts, or propolis (a sticky substance bees use like glue). The result? Smooth, clean beeswax blocks ready for DIY projects or long-term storage.

How to Render Beeswax at Home (Safely & Simply)

1. Gather Your Wax Scraps

After extracting your honey, save:

- **Cappings wax** (from uncapping your frames)
- **Broken or old comb** (free from pesticides or disease)

115

- **Leftover wax stuck to filters or tools**

Place all the wax in a **separate container**. You don't need to clean it yet—just make sure it's free of major debris like twigs or paper towels.

2. Melt the Wax Gently (Low & Slow)

Never melt beeswax directly on an open flame or hot surface—it's flammable!

Use a double boiler setup:

- Place wax in a **metal container or old saucepan**
- Put that container into a larger pot filled with water
- Heat slowly over low to medium heat

Beeswax melts at **145–150°F (63–65°C)**. Do **not** let the water boil—gentle heat ensures the wax melts without burning or separating unnaturally.

Pro tip: Always use **old pots and tools**—wax is very difficult to clean and can ruin nice kitchenware.

3. Strain Out Debris

Once the wax has fully melted, pour it through a **layer of cheesecloth** or a fine metal mesh into a clean, heat-safe container.

This step removes:

- Dead bees or bee parts
- Dirt or debris
- Residual honey or propolis

For best results:

- Fold the cheesecloth 2–3 times for finer filtration
- Place the cloth over a **wide-mouth container** (metal or silicone works great)

Important: Never pour hot wax down the sink—it hardens and clogs drains. Clean spills with paper towels while still warm.

4. Cool, Pop, and Store

After straining, let the wax sit undisturbed to cool. As it solidifies, it will form into a smooth disc or block, typically with a few dark bits at the bottom (which you can scrape off later).

Once hardened:

- Pop the wax out of the mold or container
- Store it in a **cool, dry place** away from direct sunlight
- Wrap it in parchment or a paper towel to keep dust off

Popular molds:

- Silicone muffin tins
- Cupcake trays
- Reusable soap or candle molds

A simple 4-step visual: raw wax in a bowl → melting in double boiler → straining through cheesecloth → solid wax blocks in molds

Using Beeswax in Candles, Balms, Wraps, & Crafts

Once you've rendered your beeswax (a simple process of melting and straining out impurities), you'll quickly discover just how valuable this golden byproduct truly is. Beeswax isn't just beautiful—it's **incredibly functional, sustainable, and versatile**, perfect for creating natural products for your home, body, or small business.

Whether you're making thoughtful gifts, reducing waste in your kitchen, or earning a little extra at the local farmers market, beeswax opens the door to **dozens of eco-friendly projects**.

Here's a breakdown of some of the most popular and beginner-friendly uses:

Candles – Clean-burning & naturally scented

Beeswax candles are a favorite for a reason:

- They burn longer and cleaner than paraffin (a petroleum byproduct)
- They emit **no synthetic fragrance**, just a soft, sweet, honey-like aroma
- They **purify the air** by emitting negative ions, which bind to dust and allergens
- They create a warm, golden glow that feels earthy and cozy

To make your own:

- Melt beeswax in a double boiler
- Pour into heat-safe containers or molds
- Insert a cotton wick and allow to set

Add a few drops of essential oil (lavender, orange, eucalyptus) for a gentle scent twist. These make beautiful gifts or natural home staples.

Lip Balms, Salves & Skin Care – Healing, hydrating & homemade

Beeswax acts as a natural thickener, emollient, and protective barrier in skin products. When mixed with oils like coconut, jojoba, or almond, it creates nourishing, **soothing treatments** for dry lips, hands, and heels.

Basic balm recipe:

- 1 part beeswax
- 2 parts carrier oil (like olive or almond)
- Optional: a few drops of essential oil (peppermint, tea tree, or rose)

Pour into small tins or tubes and let cool. Add herbs like calendula or chamomile for extra healing benefits.

Great for farmers market sales or thoughtful homemade care packages.

Reusable Beeswax Food Wraps – Ditch the plastic

Plastic wrap? No thanks. Beeswax wraps are washable, reusable, and beautiful alternatives made from cotton fabric infused with:

- Grated beeswax
- Pine resin (for stickiness)
- Jojoba oil (for flexibility and antimicrobial properties)

Simply iron the wax mixture into cotton cloth squares, let cool, and start wrapping your snacks, fruit, cheese, or bowls. They mold to containers using the warmth of your hands and can be used for **6–12 months**.

Eco-friendly, sustainable, and a great entry point for zero-waste living.

Wood Polish & Leather Conditioner – Shine naturally

Beeswax is excellent for making your own **wood furniture polish** or **leather conditioner**. When combined with oil (like linseed or olive), it protects and restores surfaces without the use of harsh chemicals.

For wood:

- Mix melted beeswax with oil
- Apply in small amounts with a cloth
- Buff to a clean, smooth finish

For leather:

- Use a beeswax-and-lanolin mix to soften and waterproof boots, bags, belts, and gloves

Great for woodworking hobbyists or restoring vintage items naturally.

Crafting Beyond the Basics

Beeswax's potential doesn't stop there. It's also great for:

- **Soap making** – adds hardness and skin-softening qualities
- **Crayons** – combine with pigments for non-toxic kids' art
- **Fire starters** – dip pinecones or cotton pads in melted wax for camping or fireplaces
- **Mold making, batik art, and encaustic painting** – for the artistically adventurous

Bonus: From Hobby to Hustle:

If you fall in love with these DIY projects (and many do), they can easily become **a revenue stream**. Handmade beeswax items are in demand at:

- Farmers markets

- Craft fairs
- Etsy and other online marketplaces
- Local boutiques and apothecaries

Even simple products like lip balms or tealight candles sell well when **nicely packaged and made with local ingredients**. Beeswax is a high-value product—**and it's 100% renewable from your own hive**.

Harvesting and Using Propolis and Bee Pollen

What is Propolis?

Propolis is often called "bee glue"—but it's so much more than that. Bees collect **resin from tree buds and sap flows**, then mix it with their own enzymes and wax to create this **thick, sticky substance**. They use it like caulk to seal up small cracks, smooth rough surfaces, and **sterilize the hive walls**. It even has embalming power—if an intruder like a mouse dies inside the hive and the bees can't drag it out, they'll coat it in propolis to prevent decay. Incredible, right?

For humans, propolis is a **potent natural antimicrobial**. It's long been used in traditional and modern remedies for its antibacterial, antifungal, and antiviral properties.

Common Uses of Propolis:

- **Tinctures** – Often used to support the immune system or soothe sore throats
- **Lozenges** – To ease coughs and fight inflammation
- **Skincare** – Found in creams and ointments for wounds or acne
- **Natural remedies** – Used in mouthwashes, salves, and DIY solutions

How to Harvest Propolis

Harvesting propolis is fairly straightforward and low-effort once you know what to do.

Tools Needed:

- A **propolis trap** (a flexible plastic or rubber grid with small slits)
- A **freezer**
- A **glass jar** or resealable bag for storage

Step-by-Step Process:

1. **Install the Trap:** Place the propolis trap on top of the hive, just beneath the outer cover. Bees don't like drafts, so they'll instinctively fill the tiny slits with propolis to seal airflow.
2. **Wait & Watch:** Over a few weeks, the bees will fill the trap. The timing can vary depending on the season and how much resin-producing flora is nearby.

120

3. **Freeze the Trap:** Once full, remove it and place it in the freezer for a few hours. Freezing hardens the resin.
4. **Crack & Collect:** Bend or tap the frozen trap over a clean surface. The hardened propolis will flake off like brittle shards.
5. **Store It Safely:** Keep your propolis in a clean, airtight glass jar in a cool, dark place. You can grind it later to use in tinctures or salves.

What is Bee Pollen?

Bee pollen is nature's **multivitamin in a pellet**. When bees visit flowers, they collect pollen in tiny clumps, storing it in "pollen baskets" on their hind legs. Once back at the hive, they store the pollen in comb cells and mix it with nectar and enzymes to make **bee bread**, the colony's main protein source.

For humans, bee pollen is loaded with:

- **Complete proteins** (all essential amino acids)
- **Vitamins** (especially B-complex and antioxidants like vitamin E)
- **Enzymes & flavonoids** that support health and immunity

Health-conscious people, athletes, and wellness seekers often consume it for its potential to:

- Boost energy
- Improve digestion
- Support the immune system
- Reduce inflammation

How to Harvest Bee Pollen (Carefully!)

Unlike honey, bee pollen must be harvested **thoughtfully**. Bees rely heavily on it—especially in spring and early summer—to raise their young.

Tools Needed:

- A **pollen trap** (a screen-like device fitted at the hive entrance)
- **Freezer-safe containers**

Step-by-Step Process:

1. **Install the Trap:** Pollen traps sit at the hive entrance. As foragers return home, they crawl through a fine mesh that gently brushes pollen pellets off their legs.
2. **Collect Regularly:** Check and empty the trap **every 2–3 days**. This prevents mold buildup and gives your bees a break.
3. **Freeze Immediately:** Pollen spoils quickly. Freeze your harvest immediately in airtight containers to preserve nutrients and prevent fermentation.

4. **Store with Care:** Keep frozen until use. You can consume it raw, dry it for long-term use, or blend into smoothies or granola.

Important Note:

Use pollen traps **only during peak forage times**, when plenty of blooms are available and your colony is strong. Avoid heavy collection in early spring or late fall. Over-harvesting can weaken your bees by depriving them of essential protein.

Harvesting your first honey, wax, or pollen is a thrilling milestone—but knowing how to **store each product properly** ensures that your hard work doesn't go to waste.

Safe Storage and Shelf Life of Bee Products

Different bee products have different shelf lives and storage needs. Here's a clear guide to help you **preserve quality, taste, and potency**, whether you're saving for personal use or planning to sell.

Product-by-Product Storage Guide:

Product	How to Store	Shelf Life
Honey	Keep in a clean, airtight glass jar at room temperature (no fridge needed). Store in a dark, dry place like a pantry.	**Indefinite**, as long as it stays sealed and free of moisture.
Beeswax	Store in solid blocks or sheets in a cool, dark location—preferably in paper or cloth wrap (not plastic) to allow airflow.	**Several years**; beeswax doesn't spoil, but may collect dust if exposed.
Propolis	Store dried propolis in a sealed jar away from heat and sunlight, or as a tincture in alcohol in a dark glass bottle.	**1–2 years**, especially in tincture form, if kept cool and dark.
Pollen	Place fresh or dried pollen in an airtight glass or vacuum-sealed container. Best stored in the **freezer** to preserve nutrients.	**6–12 months** in the freezer, though flavor and potency are best in first 6 months.

Quick Tips for Long-Lasting Quality:

- **Label and Date Everything**
  Always write the harvest date on every jar, block, or bottle. It helps track freshness and rotate your stock properly.

- **Keep Honey Dry**
  Honey loves to absorb moisture—but too much can cause fermentation or spoilage. Always use dry utensils when scooping.
- **Freeze Pollen Quickly**
  If not using pollen within a week or two, freeze it in a tightly sealed glass jar or vacuum bag. This preserves its nutritional value and prevents mold.
- **Protect Propolis from Light & Heat**
  Propolis is sensitive to heat and UV. Store tinctures in amber bottles and keep them in a drawer or cupboard, not on a sunny shelf.
- **Avoid Plastic for Long-Term Storage**
  While okay short-term, plastic can leach odors and chemicals over time. Opt for **glass jars**, metal tins, or paper-wrapped wax.

Bonus Tip: Crystallized Honey? Don't Panic

Honey naturally crystallizes over time, especially in cooler temps. It's still **100% edible and safe**. Just place the jar in warm (not boiling) water to gently liquefy it. Never microwave your honey—it destroys beneficial enzymes.

Wrapping up…

One of the most rewarding surprises of beekeeping is realizing that your hive isn't just a honey machine—it's a **natural apothecary**, a **craft store**, and a **pantry staple** all in one.

Whether you're melting wax, tincturing propolis, or sprinkling bee pollen on your morning yogurt, you're participating in a **centuries-old tradition of harvesting with respect** and **using every part of the hive**.

Your bees work hard—and with knowledge and care, you can honor their efforts by making the most of every golden gift they provide.

Conclusion

Take a moment to look back at how far you've come.

From learning about the life of a single honeybee to understanding the rhythm of a thriving colony...

From picking the perfect hive location to harvesting your first drop of golden honey... You're no longer just curious about bees—**you're a beekeeper in the making**.

And the best part? This is only the beginning.

More Than Just a Hobby

By now, you've likely discovered that beekeeping is more than just managing hives and collecting honey. It's about **connection**—to nature, to your food, to the seasons, and even to yourself. You're not just caring for bees; you're becoming part of a much bigger ecosystem.

As you've seen throughout this book, the act of keeping bees teaches patience, sharpens your awareness, and cultivates respect for life's smallest—and most vital—creatures.

A Lifelong Learning Experience

No matter how many books you read (and I hope this one helped!), **beekeeping is learned through doing**. Your first season may bring surprises, setbacks, and a few stings—literally and figuratively. But every hive inspection, every frame pulled, every honey harvest will build your confidence.

Trust the process. Observe your bees. Ask questions. And don't be afraid to make mistakes—because even seasoned beekeepers are still learning.

You're Never Alone

One of the beautiful things about the beekeeping world is the **community**. Local bee clubs, online forums, backyard keepers, and experienced apiarists are often more than happy to share advice, stories, and support. Bees connect people—and you're now part of that global network of pollinator protectors.

So reach out. Ask questions. Visit other hives. Attend a bee meetup. You never know how your next beekeeping breakthrough might arrive.

Your Role in Something Bigger

By starting this journey, you're not just gaining a new skill—you're helping restore balance. In a world where pollinators are struggling, every healthy hive matters. Every backyard beekeeper makes a difference.

With your care, attention, and commitment, you'll contribute to local biodiversity, food security, and the future of honeybee populations.

Your Next Steps

- Set up your first hive—if you haven't already.
- Journal your hive's behavior weekly—it's the fastest way to learn.
- Join a local beekeeping group or online community.
- Keep this book as your go-to reference guide—and come back to it often.
- And of course… **celebrate your first honey harvest** (you've earned it!).

Final Words

The bees are waiting.

They don't need you to be perfect. They just need you to show up, pay attention, and respect the incredible world they build—one cell at a time.

So zip up that suit, fire up your smoker, and step into the hum of the hive.

You're ready.

Let the adventure begin.

www.ingramcontent.com/pod-product-compliance
Lightning Source LLC
Chambersburg PA
CBHW081004140626
46546CB00019B/3361

9 781955 935654